WE'RE BACK!

The story of Stockport County's return to the Football League

By Stewart Taylor

First published in Great Britain in 2022

Copyright © Stewart Taylor 2022

Published by Victor Publishing - victorpublishing.co.uk

ISBN: 9798828310234

CONTENTS

ABOUT THE AUTHOR

Stewart is married with three children and lives near Stockport. He attended his first County match in 1975, aged eight with his Grandad who was a big Man United fan. Playing and watching football soon became an "obsession." After watching both United and County, the latter team took over and Stewart became a home and away Stockport loyalist. This provided a roller coaster experience as County flattered to deceive with brief moments of success.

His other hobby is music. Stewart has written a book on rock music and also contributed to magazines and fanzines reviewing rock albums and concerts.

Other interests include being a radio presenter. You can listen to his Classic Album Tracks Show on www.realrockradio.co.uk

Other published books include:

Back Next Year! (Stockport County) 2021

Route A666- A Heavy Metal Journey 2014

FOREWORD

It's Bob's fault. On 31st August 21 I got an email from a gentleman called Bob Thompson saying how much he enjoyed my book- Back Next Year! You may have read it. If not, the blog was an ode to the 2020/2021 season. I campaign ravaged by Covid and played almost exclusively behind closed doors. After the take-over by Mark Stott in early 2020 I became very excited about a renewed optimism around The Hatters. It didn't take long for my glass half full persona to commit to a challenge. To attend as many home and away matches as possible during the 2020/21 season. Our beloved County had become favourites for promotion back to the Football League.

With new investment the club was transformed. I was sort of a pseudo glory hunter. Ready to "invest" myself in watching all the games of a winning side. I had of course served many years of hurt punctuated with very occasional rays of football sunlight. You could say my County watching life has been more of a sporting eclipse. We've been not very good very often and very good almost never. At least over the last ten years. I ignored any glory hunter thoughts and wrote the book. Force majeure occurred and the rest is history. I got into a few matches and we eventually blew it in the play-off semi-final against the Monkey Hangers from Hartlepool.

On that day back in August 21, Bob had made my day. A lovely email which makes all the effort of writing a book worthwhile. Writing is a leap of faith. You bang away on the keyboard. Edit, read again and sometimes re-write. The text can seem good. Then a little self-doubt creeps in and you edit again. Will anybody read it? Will anyone care? As with my radio show, I always went with the ethos that if one person listens and enjoys then it is worth-while. After all, it's just all about sharing a passion.

I was nudged by kind comments to produce a second book about a County season and another bid for promotion back to the Football League. You could say the Holy Grail. A match-by-match account of the 2021/22 season. One that see's the return of fans and an opportunity for me to complete what I attempted last year. The attendance of all or most of the first team matches. Or a bloody good go at doing it. The plan being we actually get promoted this time. Fingers crossed there isn't a consecutive force majeure season!

Bob suggested I write a "sequel." Maybe call it We're Back! So here it is. I hope you enjoy and WE'RE BACK!!

INTRODUCTION

This book is a match-by-match report of the season. Intended to be unflinchingly biased of course. Being a nice guy there shouldn't be too much controversy. I am pretty level-headed so it will be full of self-deprecating humour. Humour about the football and humour about the world itself. You see, football is a leveller. It brings you back down to earth. Especially on a cold mid-week Cheshire Cup match watching County's fringe players with a few hundred other masochists. The rest of the world has gone mad anyway. It's official now. When you get to my age, things just keep getting more bizarre.

When I was a kid staring out of the window and half listening to the History teacher, I thought the world was a mad place. As the decades went by I realised the present and probably the future will keep getting madder. I am not that interested in politics or history or an expert on anything in particular (apart from obscure rock bands and random County facts). However, I wondered whether we really needed to go to the Falklands. It seemed like Iraq was the wrong country to invade. Last year I was perplexed by the trillions of dollars of equipment that was left in Afghanistan. And now Ukraine is a perplexing conundrum.

As someone once said, "in a crazy world its only your insanity that keeps you sane." Indeed this resonates with County fans and lower league club followers. You do question your sanity when attending some of the games during a season. If it ends in glory then the sanity prevails. Anything less and insanity returns. I made a quick start on insanity by the second match of the season away at Southend (more later). The great thing about being a County fan now is that we are still pinching ourselves. Are we still alive? How did we survive and are we really only dreaming? After all, up until about three years ago we had spent a decade of being the archetypal basket case club.

Now we are going from strength to strength on and off the field. All the jigsaw pieces are on the table. The border is complete and we know where the pieces need to go. All we need is for Mr Stott and his merry band of men to put everything into place and find the Holy Grail. To get us back into the football league. It is simple really. Accrue more points one way or another than any other team. I'm not even contemplating the play-off route. I need to keep my sanity for as long as possible.

In the event you are not a County fan I hope you enjoy delving into our world. Lower league fans are on tour around the outposts of football. With the dream of a Euro away day (in our case Wrexham). Or even an FA cup draw against one of the "big" boys. If you happen to be a frequenter of a Premier League or Championship team then you may find a refreshing angle to our football following life. It may bring back memories of the old days and an old school experience.

It will be a long road. There will be twists and turns, bad weather, diversions, traffic jams and frustration. Joy, boredom, celebration and anger. Many miles, highs, lows and blows. Elation, frustration and damnation. It is unlikely to be straight forward. Even though we have the benefit of funds, new players and large crowds, this is County. We never do things easily. Maybe we'll get a great start and stay at the top or maybe it will be a slow accrual of magical points. Only time will tell. One thing is for sure I will describe the action and conclusion.

Ladies and Gentlemen, let me introduce you to the mighty Stockport County and their campaign for glory in the 21/22 season! Or a match-by-match review of what happened next. I hope you enjoy and for your own sanity, keep a sense of humour at all times (just in case we balls it up).

What could possibly go wrong?

CHAPTER ONE
August 2021

Saturday 21st August 2021
County 1 Dagenham & Redbridge 3

The first match of the season. The very first match of a long campaign. When you've seen as many seasons as me, you don't get too carried away with the result. We should win today but if we lose I will definitely be more level-headed than I was when I was thirty or twenty. I approach this game in circumspect mood. The Daggers were one of the best teams to visit Edgeley Park last year.

New centre forward Scott Quigley is out injured. We go with three small players in attack. New signing Ben Whitfield, Rooney and Madden. Ben looked very lively in pre-season. I'm slightly worried about our frontline in this "massive men at the back league." There is a new back three of Fish (on loan from Man Utd), captain Hogan and new boy from Accy Stanley Ben Barclay. Barclay looked solid in pre-season. No room for Palmer or Keane.

Preparation for the match goes a bit pear shaped. The missus has blocked me in on the drive and taken her car keys with her. I can't get hold of her on the phone. The spare key opens the door but doesn't turn the ignition. A quirk of a sixteen-year-old car.

Then my son tells me at lastminute.com that he can't go because he has a shift at work. They tend to phone him at short notice. Hastily arranged substitute in place I need to get a shift on for the meet up. So I leg it to the bus. One benefit is I can have a few beers as I'm not driving. I jog from the bus station. Thirsty, I get a can of DAB lager from an off license on Castle Street. Cheap lager in hand, I receive some friendly banter.

On entry into the ground I've met up with my mate and we are pleasantly surprised that this season they've started to sell beer in the Popside. £3.50 for a bottle of Heineken but nevertheless a welcome lubricator. In a Premier League ground it would be a fiver or probably six quid down south. There are benefits to watching County.

There are an impressive 5,200 fans in the ground with a couple of hundred making the long trip from East London. A great crowd for the fifth tier of English football and bigger than some League One attendances. As a football fan impressive crowds are always a badge of honour. Edgeley Park is looking great. Mark Stott and his investment has transformed the stadium. Everything is either painted or replaced. Including new seats in the Cheadle End and Railway End. Plus an all singing all dancing new score board. Apparently the bowels of the stadium have also been transformed including the changing rooms and executive suites.

The pies are now gourmet as an upgrade from the perfunctory Hollands or Pukka pies. I had a chicken and ham and can honestly say it was delicious. Proper chicken, like something from a posh shop.

The game starts off with County on the front foot. Madden and Rooney are buzzing around like a double act. I like both but I sometimes wonder if they are playing as a team within a team. For all our frenetic play we seem incohesive. It is clear within the first ten minutes that we lack a focal point up front as in a centre forward. Ben Whitfield and Southam-Hales buzz up and down the wings but we are missing Quigley or even Reid.

Fortunately, on ten minutes Rooney fizzed a low cross from you guessed it Madden into the net to open the scoring. The game became even. We huffed and puffed. Hogan conceded what looked like a harsh free kick after handling just outside the box. The Daggers scored the free kick just before half time.

The second half followed a similar pattern as our opponents gained confidence. You could imagine their players thinking "they aren't as good as we thought they'd be!" On the hour Josh Walker slotted home for the visitors. You could imagine our players thinking "this wasn't supposed to happen, what do we do next!"

The Daggers fans start an oggy, oggy, oggy Dagenham chant. I thought this was a bit cheesy especially for East Londoners. It sounded more suitable for an Aussie sporting event or a scout camp. Two minutes later they scored again. More oggy, oggy, oggy chants. Fair play to them I suppose. I later realised this was their Digger, Digger, Dagger refrain. They scored again.

With the game over after sixty minutes we decided to discuss our performance for the last half an hour. It was one of those games where County weren't going to get back into it. We had plenty of puff but nothing up front. We could have delivered another ten crosses and no one would have been on the end of them.

The conclusion was that Scott Quigley would have made the difference. I big strong front man that could get on the end of crosses or create mayhem in the box and space for others. Reid did come on but he's not a front man. He is someone who plays off a front man and picks up the pieces.

It really is as simple as that. A group of small players up front and down the wings all dropping deep isn't effective enough in our opinion. Our manager Rusk of course is far more qualified than us!

A disappointing start and my circumspect preparation proved to be a good idea. It is great to be back though. Next stop Essex.

Saturday 28th August 2021
Southend United 0 County 1

Bank Holiday weekend. The last bank holiday of the year. Family responsibility is not quite as it used to be. Watching football gets easier when your family grows up. With small kids it really is a bit selfish to watch your team away a lot. It takes you away from family plans. I limited myself to mostly home games for a number of years. Fortunately, most of those years fell when we were truly crap.

Now the kids are leaving or have left the nest. My daughter lives in London. This weekend my eldest son is in a caravan with his mates in the Lakes and youngest son is at the Leeds music festival.

I was in two minds about this one. Firstly it is live on telly. Secondly it is a 5:20pm kick off and thirdly it is a five-hour drive away. So that's a twelve-hour mission to watch less than two hours of football involving around ten hours of driving. A bit insane really as I eluded to in the intro to this book. I struggled to get any recruits to join me in this exercise. Both lads are away and two mates dropped out. In a drinking session a couple of weeks ago, the mates were up for it. In our inebriated haze we celebrated the idea of another drinking session at the Blackpool of the South involving a cheap and cheerful B & B. Within 48 hours once sobered up, both mates decided "sod that, I'll watch it on the telly."

Sensible response really but doing things like this book is let's face it, a tad eccentric. I had no intention of doing a sequel. But subconsciously I had the thought buried deep in the grey matter. It would be good but do I have the time? Last year with everything shut during the pandemic, writing the book filled in a lot of spare time. Now, with everything back to normal, fitting in writing and editing a book is even more of a challenge than last time.

I didn't get the email from Bob Thompson until after this match so it's a good job I actually went to Southend. Bob's email was lovely and for someone to suggest that they enjoyed the first book and hoped I did a sequel was enough to ignite my enthusiasm. It doesn't take much to fill my glass!

The challenge from last year is back on. To get to as many County matches as possible. It is Essex for me. Go south my son. Then take a left turn east until you hit the Essex coast. Southend-on Sea to Roots Hall, home of Southend United FC established 1906.

So it is a solo exercise. I half considered getting the coach. Possibly the Fingerpost flyer the away match travel run for years by Lou from the Fingerpost pub. But as usual I opted for the car. I've had a company car for years so it's reliable transport door to door. Pre company cars I had several bangers including a 1974 Ford Escort that went to many away games. It had a hole in the floor near the pedals. One time coming back from Blackpool the hole let in a massive spray of water and the headlights dimmed to non-existence on the M55. It got me home though.

With automatic gears and fancy cruise control the current car is a beacon of modern automotive transport. A fairly chilled out away day option. I set off at 12pm and good job too. When you factor in comfort breaks, food pangs, all the variable speed limits and inevitable hold ups, it is a five-hour journey. It will be quicker on the late-night return though. What is certain is the satisfying albeit unhealthy eating experience. Breakfast wrap on the way down and Big Mac meal on the way back for sustenance.

Radio included Absolute Classic Rock, Talk Sport & Talk Radio. I can't decide which is more annoying; Talk Sport or Talk Radio. I've concluded both stations have a majority of plonkers as presenters. The Sport version just talks rubbish half the time. It's mainly sycophantic Premier League blather. Talk Radio, although a relief from the proliferation of woke views, veers towards right wing nonsense. The worlds gone mad and the people are going madder.

I crossed the border into Essex, then past the heartlands of Basildon. One good thing to come from there is Depeche Mode. I noticed a proliferation of obnoxious white "SUV's" trundling down the duel-carriage way. Par for the course for Essex I suppose. I got to Southend just in time. Parking was a nightmare. I straddled an entrance but didn't want to run the risk of getting wheel clamped 230 miles from home. I eventually found a spot on a residential street then jogged to the ground just in time for kick off.

We are in our new fluorescent pink third kit which replaces last season's fluorescent yellow third kit. I'm glad I've made the journey. Roots Hall is a great ground. Down each side are stands that look similar to Edgeley Park. Behind the opposite goal is a small two-tier structure. Our end has an unusual "barrel" roof. These are almost extinct. It is a thing of beauty apart from the fact it's lined with corrugated asbestos. There are cobwebs and dust everywhere. The sign of a beleaguered club. The Shrimpers are absolutely skint. They have had consecutive relegations dropping from League One. They will do well to match our nadir though!

Hogan is out as his wife is giving birth. Fish is dropped and the back three is Barclay, Keane and Palmer. Keane and

Palmer are immense throughout the match. Two genuine warriors. I didn't realise Phil Brown is the Shrimpers manager. Even from distance his famous tan is an unusual deep copper. I wondered if his whole body is that colour. I pictured a disturbing image of a deep copper head on a normal white man's body. He paces around like a caged tiger. Rusk is inanimate with only the odd shout disturbing his static body language.

County dominate the first half but we are still having problems creating clear cut chances. The "solution" is on the pitch in the form of Scott Quigley. Unfortunately, his hamstring gives up again after only twenty minutes. Reid replaces him. New loanee Raikhy from Aston Villa looks quality. He seems to glide across the pitch and delivers long passes with ease. Obvious Premier League pedigree. On fifteen minutes we go ahead courtesy of talisman Rooney. In typical fashion John dispatches a dipping drive from just outside the box that hits the in-side netting.

The 300 County fans are in fine voice, out singing the home fans. The home vocal section to the right is located as near as possible to the away fans. They rise to the challenge with a retort. Their drum rhythm matching our drum. Fair play to all the County fans who have made the long journey. We could have just watched it on the box without ten hours on the road. I realise I have only had the breakfast wrap and make my way for some half time "nutrition." The food area is an uninviting canteen with what looks like a very limited selection of "pukka" pies. They are unlikely to take cards and I shout a friendly "do you take cards love" from the queue.

The two miserable old ladies don't even look up but I notice a negative vibe in their body language. Taking it as a no I return to the stand and strike up banter with a familiar face. I can see several regulars. Some have probably not missed a match for years.

The second half was mainly a defensive exercise. The home side improved and we protected our lead. Ash Palmer was magnificent repelling attacks with towering headers. His cohort Keane was brave and equally immense. He had the scars to prove it with a head wound that required repeated treatment until he eventually adorned a head bandage. Our hero returned to the fray looking like a footballing mutant ninja turtle. The Shrimpers rattled our bar, we stood firm and played out a tense five minutes of injury time.

Rusk did a fist pump celebration at the final whistle showing a bit of personality. His team dug in deep. The players applauded the 300 nutters from Stockport. I jogged back to the car predicting how quickly I could get home. Once on board the German auto machine I "sat-naved" my way out of Sarfend on autopilot towards the M25 and back up north.

I made it back before midnight, a good half an hour quicker than the first leg of the journey. Feet up with a brew I contemplated whether it was worth it. Three points helped. I thought to myself, I've just been in a barrel roofed football stand. We've won at Roots Hall for the first time since 1977. For someone like me, that's enough.

Tuesday 31st August 2021
County 0 Grimsby Town 0

Ronaldo re-signs! My God, that's all I need. I've been putting my offspring through County conversion therapy all their lives. Admittedly we've been decidedly bang average to crap for most of their lives but I keep trying. My youngest son is a semi-convert. I'm focussing on him at the moment. He even has a season ticket. With all his other activities he won't use it for every match but he is a willing accomplice. With County on the up, the attraction of Edgeley Park has increased in the last two or three years. Last season was a bit of a wash out as the pandemic scuppered match attendance. However, the recent signings have ignited County interest in the rest of the family.

Mr Ronaldo re-signing for the Reds (the family are United sympathisers) is an attractive development. However tonight is one of those attractive matches. Grimsby are bringing an impressive 1,200 fans. They've just been relegated and represent a big club in this league. Tonight will have the biggest away following for years under spotlights with a cracking atmosphere. In fact 6,400 fans turn up. A magnificent crowd at this level.

Three points in Essex got us back on track and we expect three points tonight. The defensive three remain in place. Hogan returns to the bench after becoming a father. The main change is that Reid starts. It has been clear that we need a proper striker to start. Not sure Reid fits that bill but he's the only one we've got with Quigley injured. The opening exchanges are frenetic. There is a cracking atmosphere with both sets of supporters in fine voice.

Arjan Raikhy looked lively in midfield again. We shaded most of the first half but only created one clear cut chance. It looked like Reid should have scored. Madden fizzed a low cross along the six-yard line and Reid only had to get a touch on it. The Cheadle End was bouncing towards the end of the first half. The Grimsby fans sang Ma-ri-ners similar to the Liv-er-pool refrain. How many mariners are left in Grimsby is debatable. Mind you, there aren't many hatters left in Stockport.

The second half continued with our now familiar frenetic midfield play and the occasional great bit of wing play. With the odd cross zipped into the box but no centre forward on the end of it. Reid was disappointing again. Unfortunately for him, he is a forward who plays off a big man and in this team he gets in the way of Madden and Rooney. Once

Quigley is fit, Alex is likely to drop to the bench. In fact, if we were to make another signing, we could do with another centre forward. Bright spot was Raikhy again who was man of the match.

It started to drizzle and similar to the opening home match we didn't look like scoring towards the end. The Cheadle End kept going creating a great atmosphere. The Grimsby fans seemed happy with a point. Towards the end they serenaded us with "Stockport's a sh#thole, I want to go home." A bit cheeky considering Grimsby is no Beverley Hills. In fact, it's twin sister of Cleethorpes is the better-looking place. Which isn't saying much for Grimsby.

Decent point all in all. Great atmosphere too. Four points from three games is a tad disappointing. Four points against two of the relegated teams is ok. The opening day defeat to Dagenham was disappointing but fair play to the Daggers who were impressive. We go again.

CHAPTER TWO
September 2021

Saturday 4th September 2021
Boreham Wood 0 County 0

Boreham Wood sits on the direct line into central London. About half an hour on the train. Ideal to combine footy with a visit to see my daughter who moved to London a few months ago. For her first proper job after graduating with a first in her degree. Amazing stuff. Really proud.

I'm booked into a hotel in Boreham Wood. I've never been before. It is twinned with Elstree as far as the train station is concerned. The only fact I know is that Elstree is home to a major TV studio. Apart from that I am anticipating a bland commuter town. I'm driving down, parking at the hotel and walking to the match. After the match I'll get the train into London and back to the hotel. The trains run late so a meal in the big smoke and a few drinks are on the cards.

With the car parked up for the night, I have a chance for some pre-match beers. The plan on the way down is to find a pub with County fans in for a bit of pre-match craic. The journey down is steady away. I accrued some speeding points last summer. When the motorways were empty during lockdown the Humberside and South Yorkshire police did me for six points in a week. Literally just over the threshold on both occasions I was a tad aggrieved. I was one of a few not furloughed with special dispensation for travel. I was helping to keep the economy going while the old bill were waiting in hiding, ready to snare me.

Speeding discretions aside I have learnt that sticking to speed limits is a good way to travel. When that hot-hatch Herbert bombs past you on the M6 you are more than likely to catch up with him further down the motorway network. You ain't getting anywhere much faster on our roads.

My wife Kath would have joined me today but she has a couple of nights out in London booked soon and will see daughter Daniela. Kath does like the odd match. Her first match was the tsunami match v Walsall in the early 2000's. The game where a mini hurricane stopped play for twenty minutes while debris was cleared from the pitch. It compounded her boredom but fortunately didn't put her off forever.

Meadow Park is not bad albeit a small non-league affair. It looks new after refurbishment. The main stand has a large roof panel spelling the name of the club and the home end behind the goal is the same design with a panel declaring North Bank. I can't decide whether I like the Arsenal reference. The Gunners ladies team and Arsenal men's under-23's play here which gives the place the feel of a feeder club.

Surely this lot can't go up into the Football-League? Fair play if they do but it would be strange if they did. Ourselves, Notts County, Grimsby, Chesterfield, Southend, Wrexham not to mention Bury and Macc could still be squandering around non-league while The Wood join Sutton and Salford in League Two.

I realise the pub with County fans is in the town centre on the way to the train station. As I'm walking that way later and it's already 2:15pm I elect to blag my way into the home fans bar. No away fans allowed but I'm not wearing colours as I'm going straight to London after the match. I nod to security and look as if I'm a local. Once in the bar I sit with a pint. As kick-off approaches I wonder where their fans are. It transpires they haven't really got any. The measly attendance of about 730 includes 250 County fans. That is pretty dire and another reminder that we need to get out of this league.

We beat "The Wood" 3-0 at their Meadow Park ground last year. This season they are one of three unbeaten teams with three straight wins. The first half is one of the most boring halves of football I've ever experienced. If there was a stat for excitement this was running at 5%. Rusk seems to have a policy of keeping a clean sheet until the sixty-fifth minute, then thinks about going for the win. I'd like to remind him that if we don't score we can only get a maximum of one point. Clean sheets are good but they don't necessarily get you promoted.

We plugged away in the first half without a recognised centre forward. The first half was so crap that Rusk brought Reid on at half time. He made a difference and County finally started to put some decent moves together. We had a couple of shots on target. I moved from the terrace to the seats to get a better view of our "attacks." Our fans were getting frustrated. Jordan Keane got sight of goal. I shouted, "hit it!" Jordan was definitely in ear shot so I'll take credit. He hit a daisy cutter that rebounded off the post. Pretty much the only excitement of note. We ended up 0-0 for a consecutive match.

I'll put this one down to a decent away point. One for the connoisseur. A badge of honour for the away day follower. One that had to be endured in a long season of matches. I felt sorry for the Pompey fans sat near me. They'd come to watch a match to supplement their attendance at the England game tomorrow. They stayed to the end too. Must be real football fanatics!

Hoping for a better performance next Saturday, I walked down to the station and hopped on the train to St Pancras to meet up with my daughter. I need a beer after that performance.

Saturday 11th September 2021
County 0   Yeovil Town 3

Back at Edgeley Park today and this week I have announced to myself two new-season resolutions. Firstly to lose a few pounds. I'm slightly overweight. This may be difficult on the awaydays unless I can be bothered to make healthy packed lunches. Travelling the motorways tempts you into fast-food options at the service stations but generally I have been a good lad recently. All I've done is ban myself from Greggs, McDonalds and chippy dinners. I lost about six pounds. I fell off the wagon on the Southend trip and the massive bacon butty at Boreham Wood wasn't the best. I'll allow myself the delectation of the gourmet pies again today too. But in general I'm eating healthier.

The second resolution is to reduce or ban myself from social media. Some of the content is mad. I realise football fans are impatient and we have spent plenty of dough on the squad but our season is only four matches old. Rusk has been hamstrung (literally) by Quigley's injury. So we have to battle on and pick up points the best we can.

I know I've had a bit of a moan already about our lack of firepower but seeing as I've travelled four or five hours each way to the away matches so far I'll allow myself a bit of free speech on the subject. Most of these social media "commentators" weren't even at the matches.

The first resolution was put on hold this week with two late night works drinking and eating sessions at an exhibition at GMex (or Manchester Central in new money). Yesterday was a day off work as I manned a stand for the radio station I present for at a rock festival. Tomorrow I'm peddling my last book at the Help the Hatters programme fair. But the main event of course is today.

We should beat our opponents from Somerset. Firstly, we have better players all around the pitch. Secondly, we are now under pressure. We sit mid-table five points behind the top three. Early days but we need a confidence boost.

I was confident of a win even after recent underwhelming performances. What transpired was one of the most disastrous games of football I have ever witnessed. Everything went wrong and a section of the crowd turned on the manager and team. Where to start? The line-up wasn't right. We've had injuries and Rusk persists with three at the back. Today it all backfired. Square pegs in round holes.

To replay the calamitous collection of events may be too psychologically painful. But just a few anecdotes. Penalty given away, straight red for Ash Palmer. Some of the passes went nowhere near one of our players. In fact some went straight into touch as if they were playing rugby. Manager panics, makes changes, puts on a new forward who only arrived yesterday on loan. He screws a shot so wide with just the keeper to beat that it almost goes out for a throw in. The culprit, Kenan Dunnwald has probably played his first and last game for us. One for future County quizzes.

The start of the second half was ok. We had a go for ten minutes until Yeovil scored their second. To be fair the Glovers played well but we made it easy. With the team devoid of ideas, a section of the crowd sang gallows humour chants to their own players. Then, as the management team were devoid of any solution, a fan stands next to the bench berating Rusk and McGhee. I wouldn't have done that as it is out of order and McGhee is known for his short temper and fighting fans.

In a surreal finish to the game we just sat there at the end for a few minutes in bemusement. It was the kind of game which gets a manager sacked. The players played as if they had never seen each other before. Yeovil couldn't believe their luck. It could have been worse. They nearly got a fourth.

I am putting this one in a little file to hide away. The crappest performances ever file. We've just got to move on from this debacle. At least I sold a few books the next day at the programme and memorabilia faire at Edgeley Park.

I've bought my ticket for Tuesday already so there's no going back now. A long journey to Berkshire after an extremely dodgy home performance. One for the connoisseur. However, it could be one not to be missed. It's a funny old game as Jimmy Greaves used to say. Through adversity comes opportunity. Or something like that.

Keep the faith!

Tuesday 14th September 2021
Maidenhead 0 County 2

I am combining this one with work. As I visit construction sites and clients I have the flexibility to choose a location which can usually coincide roughly with the geographical location of the match. Or in honest terms; any old excuse to go somewhere near the match.

On arrival in sunny Maidenhead (a rather pleasant part of Berkshire somewhere near Reading) I alighted at my utilitarian chain hotel. Without naming which chain, I had the comfort in knowing that these places guarantee some basic features. Such as showers that work, telly's that provide a clear picture, beds that are comfortable and a menu that serves the same thing at each branch to a decent standard. You know what you are going to get- no surprises.

I have however stayed in numerous hotels over the years that flatter to deceive. Usually independent type places that may cost a fair bit but fail badly in various departments. Establishments that are in beautiful locations or boast architectural features. Everything is good until you kick back on the bed and the telly doesn't work. Or the picture is a grainy image. You then realise that although the hotel is nice the TV is from 1992. The other annoyance is the low-pressure shower or the shower that changes temperature every two minutes.

Using the amazing google maps app I punched Maidenhead United FC into my all singing all dancing communication device. The ground is just 0.6 miles through the town centre and my arrival time is estimated at 7:40pm. I tried to gain access through the front of the stadium. Only to be told away fans are the other way- first left and left again. As it transpired first left was actually about five hundred yards past the shops and then first left back parallel to where I came from. I tried a cut through to no avail. A bunch of County fans jogged past me presumably in the same predicament.

Inside York Road just in time for kick off, I was immediately cheered up by the sight of Mark Kitching. A surprise return from his long injury lay-off. A decent throng of approximately 250 County fans are here. Another long journey for the committed. The Hatters dominated the opening exchanges by attacking the Magpies relentlessly for fifteen minutes. This is more like it. An impressive counter-attack involving Madden, Reid and Will Collar eventually saw Collar burst into the area from deep and tee up John Rooney to slam home his third of the campaign. Class football. Soon after, Maidenhead defender Remy Clerima received his marching orders following a stamp on Will Collar in a bizarre goal mouth incident.

Not long after halftime Mark Kitching, so impressive on his return to the side, whipped a corner in from the right with Reid on hand to nod past a helpless Holden. Holden got his marching orders not long after when he nearly decapitated Reid as Reid chased a ball down into the box. With the Magpies down to nine men County continued to dominate managing the game well to get the three points.

Great night and I chatted with some of the County regulars. Also a couple of County exiles who live down south. One guy who's in the RAF showed me his photos from the recent evacuations from Baghdad. The Maidenhead fans were good all game. Loud when at the other end. Then they came down our end at half time as Maidenhead were kicking our way in the second half. A great feature of non-league. The ability to change ends at half time at some grounds. Excellent banter followed between the fans.

Three points on the road and everything seems a lot rosier in the County garden. Hopefully, these shoots of recovery blossom into a beautiful three points at the Shay on Saturday as County make the short journey to Halifax. A few County fans described a slow journey to the game on the coach. It was a slow one back by all accounts. Fortunately for me, I had a spring in my step as I walked the short distance to my chain hotel home.

Saturday 18th September 2021
Halifax Town 3   County 0

At last a local away game. In fact this is the closest away game of the season bar Altrincham. In the past we've had a proliferation of local derbies. Back in the Championship, League 1 and League 2 days we would have an array of North-West rivalries such as Bury, Oldham, Bolton,

Macclesfield, Preston, Blackpool, Wigan, Burnley, Crewe, Rochdale etc. Plus Port Vale and Stoke a quick dash down the M6. Even Rotherham, Barnsley and Sheffield were a picturesque short jaunt over the Pennine moors. Now we find ourselves in a mainly southern league making long treks to non-league outposts. The joy of footy fanaticism.

This season we look forward to the nearest destinations. They still put a few miles on the tachometer. I'm thinking Halifax, Alty and maybe Wrexham. That's about it. After that we are considering Notts County, Chesterfield and Grimsby as local-ish! Welcome to the long-distance division also known as the National League. Today, rather than the 250-350 hardy souls at our first three long distance away games, there should be around 1,000 Hatters fans. I'm with a mate for this one. Jonnie is working. Fair play to my lads-they are workers as well as students. The two can co-exist!

This will be a proper test. Halifax are decent. They are candidates for the play-offs. This may be their biggest crowd of the season so it's all set up for a cracker. Halifax have decided to make it cash only pay on the gate. If there is good weather we may get a surge of Stopfordians. However, the Shaymen are charging £21 which is a bit steep.

Kath is away in London this weekend on a ladies jolly. It is debatable who will consume the most alcohol. They had rather large bottles of prosecco to lubricate the train ride down. I took the opportunity to have several beers last night. Today is a reasonable eleven quid on the train to West Yorkshire. We got on at the end of my road, enjoyed a pint at Victoria station and a couple of cans en route. A sunny journey through Rochdale, Todmorden and Hebden Bridge with good chats shared with other County fans. A few more were supped in the Three Pigeons near Halifax station. A great real ale pub. Proper away day with beer and sun.

The atmosphere in the away end was loud pre-kick off and continued through-out the first half. Fantastic support by the

Hatters fans. Unfortunately the first half got progressively worse on the pitch. We started ok dominating possession and had a couple of chances. One bouncing off the bar and another clipping a post. Fine margins. With a bit of luck, one would have gone in and it could have a been completely different game. Just before half time Hogan gave away a silly free kick just outside our box. Ex-County player Matty Warburton converted the dead ball just inside the post. County goalie Hinchliffe should have done better.

That goal obliterated our confidence. We didn't see a reaction. In fact the second half was similar to the debacle last week against Yeovil. The players miss-hit passes and looked like strangers. Rusk and McGhee looked devoid of ideas. In the seventy-eighth minute the inevitable happened when Bradbury doubled the hosts tally. Our defence looked all over the place. To add insult to injury another dis-organised response to a Halifax attack resulted in a third goal in injury time.

Apparently there were "only" 900 County fans in attendance. Last week's debacle putting a few hundred off. The support was superb until mid-way through the second half when a large proportion of our fans started to turn against the team and manager. Consecutive 3-0 defeats have almost extinguished any support for Rusk. The players need looking at too but the manager will be the one that gets the chop. Another performance like this at home against Wrexham will more than likely result in a change of management. Not what we want but this team is not performing anywhere near its potential.

Overall though it was a great away day. We had a couple of more pints in Halifax before a final one in the Northern Quarter in Manchester. It was brilliant to have a local away day and the sun shone. Life is ok. I just need my football team to start performing. It's getting a bit embarrassing now.

Saturday 25th September 2021
County 2 Wrexham 1

I'm past trepidation when it comes to County. I've seen some incredible highs and consistent lows. Multiple relegations and a ten-year period marooned in non-league. Our Welsh opponents have spent an incredible fourteen years in the National League. We went one better spending several years in the league below. It is make or break for Rusk today. Surely the project is broken if we lose again. Consecutive 0-3 losses against inferior opposition (on paper) have left the Hatters fans perplexed. Infuriated in the main. Those losses followed a series of other unconvincing performances.

Wrexham are playing well after the Hollywood effect of their new owners enabled the only professional club in North Wales to recruit quality players. They have gelled. We have gone backwards. We have the best squad in the league. However, poor tactics and evaporating team spirit have thrown the project into a tailspin. Jonnie and I are keeping the faith. Giving Rusk one more chance as we take our seats. For most the manager is past redemption. Only our director of football Simon Wilson could possibly find any reasons for optimism from this seasons performances. Rusk was his appointment. They need to make it work.

The Red Dragons sold out their 1,700 allocation in twenty minutes. The rumour is a few hundred Wrexham fans have bought seats in the home areas. A recipe for trouble. If County have a bad start to the match this could turn toxic. Hopefully not. The players need to show up. If not in support of Rusk, in support of themselves and the fans. Fingers crossed, today will be the big turnaround for our season.

Rumour of a mass Welsh invasion is unfounded. Thankfully, they haven't infiltrated our part of the Popside. The atmosphere is electric as the County fans get behind the team from kick-off. Part support/ part defiance I suspect.

Ross replaces Hinchliffe. Our regular keeper has been below par recently giving Ross a chance.

Shockingly, after only 52 seconds the visitors stunned us. A long clearance by goalkeeper Ron Lainton, found Paul Mullin. Wrexham's headline summer capture from Cambridge United made no mistake – dinking the ball over Ross and into the net at the Railway End. Unfortunately, the pattern of play is similar to this seasons theme. Our small-ish forwards up against the usual defensive giants in this league. Their number five is dominating anything that comes near him. The support from the Cheadle End is superb but the first half ends on a typically disappointing note.

Not sure what Rusk said in the changing rooms but the team are sent out several minutes early for the second half. A second half that could be the big turnaround for our season. We were excellent in the second period. Whitfield in particular demonstrating an immense effort. Ben never stopped and was all over the pitch. Hogan, Palmer, Kitching and Croasdale were the other standouts in a great fight back. Madden headed home a Rooney corner three minutes after the break. County dominated and sub Rydel scored our second late on with a tap in from some rebounding action in the box.

Most of the bumper crowd of 7,700 celebrated at the final whistle. The players looked relieved. They put a big shift in and hopefully this is the rebound effect we are looking for. We walked back to the car chuffed to bits. One of the benefits of following a lower league team or any team that doesn't expect success, is that the good bits are that much sweeter.

CHAPTER THREE
October 2021

Saturday 2nd October 2021
Weymouth 1 County 2

As mentioned in the last book – Back Next Year!- following a football team home and away for a full season is eccentric at best bordering on insane. Especially considering the long distance away destinations in this league. I had booked a hotel in Weymouth and convinced Kath and Jonnie that the Dorset beach resort was a must-see treat. With a County match thrown in. Weymouth is indeed a nice place. Voted by some as the best beach in the UK. I've never been but it looks nice on a google search.

I changed plans when I remembered that I am driving down to Bristol in the middle of the week with work. To travel the same route a few of days later wasn't particularly enticing. Plus five hours each way in two days to Weymouth is a long jaunt for Kath and Jonnie. The train is out of the question requiring an expensive and slow journey with several changes.

The only sensible solution is to sack it off. But what if County go up and I could have continued this blog to a glorious conclusion? Is that possible considering our not too impressive start? There you go, I've even started talking to myself! I toyed with the idea of going. Should I drive, should I get the coach. Utter madness. However the pull was too much, I need to continue this quest. The Wrexham victory re-invigorated my enthusiasm.

I've decided I am going to do it. It's a bit mad but after the premise of the last book was scuppered by a pandemic, I feel the need to attend as many matches as possible to reflect the planned experience. Volume 2 you could call it. One for some County fans or lower league connoisseurs. I'll drive.

There are benefits to these long-distance adventures. You meet some great people apart from the usual loyalists. At Maidenhead I met the RAF guy from Cirencester who had just come back from Kabul. His Dad is from Hazel Grove and he attends our southern matches. He showed me his photos of the recent air lifts from the runway. At the same game there was a young guy called Ruben Clark who is writing a book about lower league teams and the fan experience. He is following County, Ashton United and Mossley this season.

Ruben has already watched 25 matches this season in research for his book. He is on course for 500 pages of content that he admits will need editing. I thought I was going to unusual lengths. But there are others out there such as Ruben on a quest too. He has a website blogging his journey. His writing is excellent and the book will be too.

This is a same day return. I did the same for Southend so it isn't that bad. A coffee re-charge on the return journey should do the trick. I reminded myself that Plymouth or Newcastle fans must do similar on a regular basis.

County have another new recruit this week. Highly rated winger Ollie Crankshaw from Bradford City. Newby goes out on a month's loan to Halifax as his first team chances have dwindled further. Mark Stott has stepped down from his temporary Chairmanship now he has found his permanent replacement. Robert Elstone is the man. He was CEO at

Everton and Rugby Super League. Stott can now concentrate on his business and leave the football "expertise" to Robert. Fingers crossed this works.

The Bob Lucas Stadium is an out-of-town ground built in 1987. Bob was an ex-player, president and physio for an impressive 1,750 games. A decent-sized stadium. The away end is fortunately covered. Most of the paint is peeling away from the stanchions and crash barriers on the terrace. The rain is coming down like stair rods. I was a bit worried it might get called off after a 250-mile journey.

Fryers is injured meaning 18-year-old Ethan Pye gets a debut. New boy Crankshaw is on the bench. County start lively as usual until we fall into our all too disappointing pattern. That being a lot of huffing and puffing with a big gap in midfield which the opposition exploit. Coupled with a recent penchant for miss-placed passing it doesn't look promising.

The Terras should have scored on twenty minutes. It looked a goal but was chalked off for off-side. Our hosts made sure about twenty minutes later when Hogan and Ross had a terrible mix up resulting in a tap in. I very disgruntled away end trundled off to the bogs and concession hut at the break.

Second half was a massive improvement. Madden in particular got going with the assistance of the consistent Southam-Hales. But it wasn't until new signing Crankshaw entered the fray that we looked like equalising. Our new winger fed Southam-Hales who fizzed a low cross in for Madden to slide into the net. Madden had another disallowed for off-side. Then in the last minute another cross from Southam-Hales found our new hero Crankshaw to tap in. The away end went mental. Our new boy looked a cut above the rest and must start at home to Aldershot next Saturday.

Other results go for us and we now sit just six points off top spot. Another Rusk reprieve. With Minihan, Keane and

Quigley back from injury soon, we may start to look like a promotion candidate.

The return journey was a pleasure rather than a chore with three points in the bag. It took "only" four and a half hours. It even stopped raining.

Saturday 9th October 2021
County 1 Aldershot 0

After an unusually dry and warm September, reality has kicked in meteorologically. The temperature has dropped recently and it has started to piss it down on a regular basis. Match days up until the end of September were shirt sleeve affairs involving dry and pleasant travelling conditions. Last week's pilgrimage to Weymouth was wet. But we are used to it and just need to be reminded of our weather reality. Following a team all season involves a sport played mainly in the winter and autumnal months.

Today we have the Shots as opponents who lie second bottom in the league. Only the points deducted Dover prevent them from being rock bottom. I have been waxing lyrical about new boy Crankshaw to Jonnie all week. This combined with our lowly opposition has resulted in a positive score prediction contest as we take our seats. I'm going 3-0, Jonnie says 2-1. Maybe slightly optimistic from me and Jonnie with a sensible alternative. After all, he has only attended the home games up to now where we have been particularly generous to the opposition.

Crankshaw did look good though when he came on at Weymouth. He speeded up our attack. Much needed after some of our laborious build ups this season.

Contrary to my meteorological update, the temperature has decided to increase to a "balmy" seventeen degrees with only 40% chance of rain in the second half. There are plenty of kids in the Popside and it is great to see. The future of County. The ground looks great and another impressive crowd of over 6,100 is in attendance. It is all good off the pitch at the moment. Events on the pitch are slowly going in the right direction. Two wins on the bounce with a winnable game today.

Good news is Scott Quigley is back on the bench, Jordan Keane has also returned from injury and starts alongside Palmer with Hogan as a sub. County look threatening with Whitfield looking dangerous. On the other side home debutant Crankshaw and Southam-Hales look impressive as a wide attacking combo. We still look disjointed overall.

Jonnie makes the same comments as most fans. "There's no link between midfield and the forwards." "There's a big hole in midfield." "We keep humping long balls up to little forwards." "We look great down the wings but then there's no one in the middle."

Mr Rusk and your significant entourage of support staff, these issues are as plain as the nose on your face. Fortunately just before half time, Madden is unmarked at the back post and heads home from a Whitfield cross. Good job as for all our possession we let the Shots in for a few scares. Ross made a good save and they hit the woodwork.

The second half looked like Rusk had settled for the 1-0 early after the break. A risky policy and the Shots again had several chances hitting the woodwork again. One bright spot was the introduction of Quigley after injury. Crankshaw had an impressive home debut and Keane was man of the match. He is the one that can carry the ball from defence. I would consider him to occupy that hole we have in midfield.

Can't complain with three wins in a row but entertainment was at a premium in the second half. If we win our game in hand we are in the play-off spots. Steady progress. Far from convincing as a cohesive unit but we have so many quality players that surely everything should click into place soon.

At the end, a pitch invader jogs across the pitch and looks a bit lost until Scott Quigley guides him off. Alcohol was probably involved. He entered from the Cheadle End. Those two-pint beers in the CE bar would likely provide evidence.

Saturday 16th October 2021
FA Cup Fourth Qualifying Round
County 3 Stamford 0

Cup action today against Stamford who reside near Peterborough in Lincolnshire. They are nicknamed the "Daniels" after Daniel Lambert, often cited as England's heaviest ever man, a Stamford resident. They are two or three levels below us in the pyramid so this will be our opponents "cup final." They will be looking for a giant killing in front of a big crowd and a big pay day. There should be around 3,000 fans here. The club have only opened two stands for home fans: the Cheadle End and Main Stand. I generous ticket tariff of only six quid for adults and a quid for kids is a great gesture by the club. The proceeds are split 50/50 so Stamford will get a well-earned financial reward.

As our usual season ticket abode in the Pop Side is shut, we've decided on the Main Stand. I've only ever been in the Main Stand a few times so we have decided that we will check this view out. Normally we would go for the Cheadle End but it's good to have a change.

This is a chance for Rusk to pick from his significant squad. We must have the biggest squad in the league. A few are on loan such as Newby but there is still a big pool to select from.

I predict that the likes of Keane, Fish, Hinchliffe, Rydel, Barclay, Raikhy, Collar, Reid will all start. With Quigley who needs to get match fitness. Maybe even some youth players on the bench. You look at that list and we could field two teams that should be able to compete in the National League. With our resources we should be in the top two. That's another topic as today is the cup. It is always good to watch a knock-out match.

A healthy 3,000 fans as predicted turned up with 120 travelling from South Lincs. The Daniels put up a decent showing but couldn't deny Croasdale who finished off a nice move with a side footer on the half hour mark. We got a great view from our Main Stand location. This stand is the best view in the house. Second half Madden converted a penalty to keep his run going and Quigley completed the scoring with a header. Quigs came off the bench to score his first County goal. A much-needed option now he has returned from injury.

Most of the players mentioned got a look in with Raikhy tidy on the ball. Keane was a stand-out and Croasdale man of the match. Rooney was rested but came on from the bench with Reid. County were tidy and controlled play with patience. The three goals came as expected. Not a blow me away performance but satisfactory as we keep the winning habit going.

Into the First-Round proper and our ball got pulled out of the bag with Bolton. A plumb tie to look forward to in a couple of weeks.

Tuesday 19th October 2021
Cheshire Senior Cup
Chester 0 County 1

County play forty-four league matches so that's twenty-two on the road. We are in three cup competitions- the FA Cup, FA Trophy and tonight's fixture in the Cheshire Senior Cup. Some Premier League teams play in Europe, the FA Cup and League Cup. That takes some commitment too. My quest is around England and one flirtation across the border to Wrexham (unless we get them or another Welsh team in the FA Cup). I'm enjoying the challenge.

Tonight is a relatively short journey to the other side of Cheshire. In a competition that most County fans aren't bothered about. It is a chance to check out fringe players and youngsters. I'm so keen on watching County that I'm up for this as well as it being one to complete the season. Although I doubt I'll repeat this in the future.

I'm with a Liverpool supporting Chester sympathiser tonight. An old work mate and footy nut. He lives just over the border in North Wales and we meet up pre-match for a pint. John hasn't made the big club to small club conversion. He has threatened for years regaling me with tales of dissatisfaction with modern corporate football. Especially the eye watering ticket prices at Anfield. Several years ago he was paying nearly £800 for his season ticket. That didn't include any cup tickets either. After fan demonstrations the club stopped increases for a period.

I never went to the old Sealand Road ground. Photos suggest it was a decent size old school affair. The club sold it and with the cash built the new one in 1992 on an industrial estate. The entrance is literally on the border with Wales. This was one of the first phase of new grounds that started in the late eighties/ early nineties. Until then all teams played in their original stadiums. Most a hundred years old. I am sure Chester were happy with their shiny new stands in 92. But it is a disappointing affair. Devoid of character on an industrial estate. Four small boxes for stands with a box stuck on the front for the offices.

Seeing as we have a massive squad there will be wholesale changes tonight. There were indeed changes in the line-up. Most notably Millenic Alli a tricky winger who was the standout player. Coming on as a sub he ran at defenders. Culminating in a mazy dribble and powerful burst of speed past a defender into the box before drilling the ball home for the only goal of the game. Great finish resulting in a somersault celebration in front of the County faithful.

Worth the journey just for Millenic's goal, I drove home a satisfied supporter. There were only 350 people there with half from Stockport. One for the connoisseur. I got a bit of a buzz as I calculated that this was five wins in a row and seven in eight. Two victories were in cups and we haven't looked convincing but nevertheless progress.

We are on the up but a sterner test lies ahead in Nottinghamshire on Saturday.

Saturday 23rd October 2021
Notts County 2 County 1

We've sold 1,700 tickets to set up a fantastic match between two promotion favourites. Jonnie is loving the idea of a big away match. Some of our fanbase are loving the idea of a visit to Hooters in Nottingham. Social media has many Hooters posts. A rather tame eatery with you got it, scantily clad young waitresses. I've been to one in the States. There are only a couple in the UK apparently.

This match is about as big as I want. This season has increased my apathy for the Premier League. The fans are used and abused but many fans are willing to put the blinkers on. They should be biting the bullet and walking away. Find a lower league club where the fans are appreciated. A United supporting mate has just informed me that all three December away games (Norwich, Brentford and Newcastle) have been rescheduled for TV meaning missing the last trains back. While the selectively performing Pogba is holding out for £450k a week!

Meanwhile up at the Toon, the manic looking Amanda Staveley heads up a quango including dodgy Saudi financing. They are getting the Sky TV thumbs up, presumably until the inevitable ESL (European Super League) breakaway rears its ugly head again. Then Sky will be tendering for the rights. While in Saudi, women can't drive, torture in jails is standard and journalists that step out of line get chopped up. Give me County any day.

Back to real footy, there is a massive buzz walking into the ground. In the last book I wasn't overly complimentary about Meadow Lane. I have been a few times but the pandemic scuppered last season's attendance. This time I'm here in the flesh and I can confirm from the outside it is like a big Chester. Four boxy breeze block structures on an industrial estate. Once inside though the ground comes to life and is an impressive size. It is a 20,000 capacity Championship ready facility. In fact it would be ok in the Prem. Notts really shouldn't be in this league and neither should we. Both of us are going to do everything possible to escape starting this afternoon.

The big pre-match news is we have signed Bolton captain Antoni Sarcevic on a free. A recent fallout with his manager at Wanderers has resulted in their loss and our gain. Another statement of intent by our beloved owner Mark Stott.

From the offset this game was a damp squib. After a recent run of victories in winnable games County again failed against a top ten team. Quigley is now back but we still look the same. Laboured and devoid of any real shape. Dependent on individual moments. Notts played ok but nothing special.

Danger man Wootton finished nicely on the volley for Notts just after half time. They scored again and with twenty minutes to go we still didn't look like scoring. Only a ninety fourth minute penalty conversion by Whitfield registered anything for the Hatters. Fans almost came to blows around us arguing about Rusk and Gannon and the management situation in general. Some of the players body language was poor. Rooney had a terrible game. He was good last season. Reid scored twenty goals last season. This year he has one and hasn't looked like scoring again.

As we enter the winter period, Rusk is skating on very thin ice. Surely Stott and new Chairman Robert Elstone must be reviewing the managers tenure. After massive investment we languish tenth, twelve points behind top spot. The football isn't very entertaining and the fans have lost faith. Let's hope Mr Rusk turns it around but the odds are against it.

The next three league games are very winnable: Barnet, Dover and Bromley. Anything less than seven points is unacceptable.

Tuesday 26th October 2021
County 1 Barnet 2

Another debacle of a match. Simon Rusk and assistant Mark McGhee were relieved of their duties the morning after this game. It had got to the stage that the instigators of a new "culture" at the club had to admit defeat. Their experiment has failed. Fans would also like Simon Wilson (Director of Football) to go too. That is highly unlikely as he was appointed by our owner Mark Stott. New Chairman Robert Elstone will have a say in the appointment of a new manager along with Wilson.

It has been less than a year since the club sacked club legend and manager Jim Gannon. County were in fourth place in the table with games in hand. We had just matched West Ham for eighty minutes in the FA Cup. There was no reason to sack Jim. The club gambled on Rusk and lost.

An 18-match unbeaten run including a lot of draws was the only "achievement" in the Rusk tenure. We never beat a top six team. We hardly put up a fight in the play-off semi-final defeat at the end of last season. The football wasn't very exciting. This season the entertainment levels dipped further. Recently some players looked to have given up. If we the fans can see the lack of tactics the players will be just as frustrated. It is now surely time to select a manger with experience at this level rather than a promising U-23 coach.

The Barnet game followed a similar pattern to the Notts County match. A few players putting a shift in while the rest looked unrecognisable to their potential performance levels. Our opponents were just above the relegation zone while we have by far the biggest and most expensive squad in the league. On the pitch there was no gap as Barnet matched us. Widdowson scored after twenty minutes. Near the end Southam-Hales uncharacteristically received a red card after a two footed challenge on the Barnet scorer. County equalised with a nice goal from Crankshaw who latched on to a great ball by home-debutant Sarcevic just before half-time.

Barnet won the match just after the break from a corner. The current County don't look like a side that can come back from behind and they didn't. Terrible night. So bad, the club had to admit defeat and conclude their experiment with

Rusk. All we can hope for now is a complete turnaround in form under interim manager Dave Conlon.

A sense of foreboding crept over me. Even an optimist like myself couldn't muster anything positive from tonight. Maybe Crankshaw's goal. Other than that, the playing side of the club has become a complete mess. How long will this continue? Fortunately, the club made changes the next day and we can only wish for rapid improvements.

One bright spot is that the club have sold all 4,000 allocated tickets for the FA Cup game at Bolton. A magnificent effort by the Hatters faithful, especially considering our recent form. Now it is time for the club to repay our loyalty.

Saturday 30th October 2021
Dover Athletic 2 County 5

In the last book I said Dover was only 31 miles (27 nautical miles) from Calais and 300 miles from Stockport! The Fingerpost Flyer coach does a return trip of 600 miles in the same day. That is a hell of a journey for two hours of football in front of about 900 fans up a hill in Dover. That coach trip starts at 7am and concludes around midnight. I doff my cap to all on board.

The Whites of Dover are down already. Docked twelve points they sit at a minus nine-point tally and rock bottom. Last season the pandemic side-blinded them. The part-time club located on the very edge of the country was hit as bad as any team. Chairman Jim Parmenter claimed carrying on with no fans and the overhead required to operate would send them into liquidation. He decided to furlough his team and play youth players but eventually went on strike.

Their results up to that point were expunged including County's home win. He should have just carried on with youth players as relegation was cancelled for the season. He didn't, the club got docked twelve points for this season and a £40,000 fine. He refused to pay the fine and Dover are doomed. They have only drawn three with no victories after eleven matches. Surely we will win this game. Especially considering the bounce back teams get from a change in management.

I'm giving this one a miss. I've been to Dover before with work. It is a working town dedicated to ferries (stating the obvious). I stopped over once. There are a few olde maritime pubs and that's about it. Nothing to particularly entice an overnight stay. The drive is torturous. I have a better offer in a warm pub tonight so this will be the first match I listen to on Strawberry Radio (County's dedicated commentary service).

I've ticked off the five-hour Weymouth journey. Dover is for the real nutters. Of course, if we get an uber-long-distance destination in the play-offs I will have to attend. Anyhow, the team barely deserves the loyalty at the moment. I've decided I'd rather be in the pub than stuck on the M2/M25/M1/M6/M56 etc. To further satisfy my reasoning I've just returned from Newcastle after a visit to my eldest son who is at the Uni. Plenty of miles on the clock already this week.

A comforting development is the County-centric appointment of an interim management team. Dave Conlon is joined by Michael Raynes and James Jennings. At last we get some real County feel about proceedings. After Rusky the U-23 coach, veteran McGhee and god knows who behind the scenes, at least we have three real County people at the helm. For the moment at least until the club announce the new permanent manager. Surely, this time, the nominee will have experience of the National League.

It is nice to hear the dulcet tones of County commentary stalwart Jon Keighren on Strawberry Radio. I've heard that even the uber-loyalist Keighren has been questioning Rusk and the club recently. When Jon starts losing faith you know things are bad. Things are bad and there is no guarantee they will get better straight away. Hopefully, this is just a chapter in the story of our glorious return to the football league.

At the Crabble, County kick off in all pink. We get a fortuitous opener from Quigley. The ball rebounds off his foot more than it being an actual shot. We'll take it though. The commentary connection goes down replaced by Strawberry Radio greatest hits. Hoping the same doesn't happen in my radio show tonight. Mines pre-recorded so should be ok. A ten- minute commentary silence ensues.

Dover are better than expected and equalise from a pen as Hogan fouled unnecessarily. In a change from our usual cautious tactics under Rusk, County are more expansive. So are Dover with nothing to lose in their predicament. The Hatters finish the half strongly and just before the break Madden smashes home from close range.

The Whites equalise early in the second half before we go ahead again through Crankshaw. 3-2. County should have put this game to bed by now after numerous chances. We do when Hogan plants a header into the back of the net for a fourth goal with 15 mins to go. Then it's five when Whitfield taps one in at the death. By far a perfect performance but three precious points in the bag.

Dave Challinor was announced as manager of Stockport County on the Tuesday evening with an interview by Jon Keighren. Absolutely amazing news. Unanimous acceptance by the County fan base. Dave is an ex-County player and has an excellent track record in management with Colwyn Bay, Fylde and Hartlepool. Nothing is guaranteed but this should put our season back on track.

CHAPTER FOUR
November 2021

Sunday 7th November 2021
FA Cup First Round
Bolton Wanderers 2 County 2

The Trotters play the Hatters in a local derby. Both teams have fallen from a great height in recent history. Bolton looked over the precipice while County well and truly dropped off it. In ten years Bolton dropped from the Premier League to League Two. While in a ten-year period County dropped from the Championship to National League North. Both teams are now on a resurgence making for a great FA Cup draw.

Today there are 5,000 of the Hatters hordes in attendance. Jonnie is playing in a match so I have recruited a mate. This is probably our biggest ever away following outside Wembley appearances. With new manager Dave Challinor in place this game has become even more exciting. A sense of stability has been introduced. Dave has experience at National league level and as a player in the Football League. Today is a free shot against a League 1 club.

Our destination isn't technically in Bolton, it's in Horwich. Closer to Chorley or even equidistant to the centre of Wigan (which must really annoy their fans). I'm old enough to have visited Burnden Park their characterful old ground near Bolton town centre. Even though the new one suffers from it's out of town location, the stadium itself is one of the best examples of a new era ground. Rather than a boxy affair the stands are arched into four curves similar to Huddersfield's ground. I've lost track of the stadiums various naming descriptions. It is now the University of Bolton stadium. Another strange development whereby any town can now claim a University.

As we arrive at the ground, it feels like we are back in the big time. Relative to the last ten years at least. Visits to this place, Molineux, Ewood Park, Maine Rd, the City Ground, Hillsborough, the Hawthorns, Selhurst Park etc were our standard away days twenty years ago. Not wearing colours, we blagged our way into the nearest pub for home fans only. Soon a group of disgruntled County fans were arguing with the pub manager having somehow entered in County shirts. Smelling trouble we left for the ground. We got a pint on the concourse inside the ground.

Our end of the stadium is absolutely packed out. The atmosphere is electric. This season is taking a turn for the better. I must admit I was losing faith in the possibility of writing a book about a promotion season. Under Rusk things went a bit turgid. Almost to the point where there was little optimism of going up even after only ten games. Now anything seems possible. Most fans are quietly confident of an upset against our League 1 hosts. It is early days though-Dave Challinor hasn't even been in charge for a game yet. However, his interviews and track record in promotions in nearly every season he's been a manager are providing a massive confidence boost.

The game was a cracker. County pressed and attacked better than anytime under the Rusk regime. Every player performed. Quigley was phenomenal and scored early on. Bolton fought back to take the lead before a lovely move resulted in Whitfield equalising on half time. 2-2 and a brilliant half of football. The second period was a cagier affair but we still had chances. Quigley broke away on a run one on one with the keeper and just pushed the ball too far. 3-2 would have been epic.

The fans were excellent. Several blue and white flares greeted our goals adding to the spectacle. We were loud and proud. The biggest away following of the weekend in any league or cup match in the country. The largest away following in the history of the FA Cup First Round. Great banter with the Bolton fans near us. A perfect away day.

In a poignant moment, a minutes applause took place for a young County fan who passed away recently. The Bolton fans honoured George Thompson impeccably too. In a crowd of 5,110 County fans I was coincidentally stood next to George's Grandad. A moving occasion. Later I wondered if his name was Bob. Bob Thompson who sent me the email.

Last time I was here was about twenty years ago when we won 1-0 in Div 1 (now the Championship). This time it feels like a new start for County. The performance was positive and entertaining. Our new manager is like a breath of fresh air. We are on telly on Saturday against Bromley. Followed by a live BBC match next Wednesday for the replay versus Bolton at Edgeley Park. The draw has been made and the winner plays Rotherham away.

Saturday 13th November 2021
County 1 Bromley 1

This is a BT live match – a 5:20pm kick off. We are back on telly on Wednesday in the FA Cup too. I have a tinge of excitement. This might be one of those seasons. Media exposure in the league and cups with live TV coverage.

Potentially a quick move up towards the top of the league. If it is anything like the seminal 96/97 season we are in for a famous campaign. 96/97, if anyone needs reminding, was our promotion to the Championship year with a run to the semi-final of the League Cup. Plenty of TV coverage where County came to the nation's attention in a big way.

Last week with our mega 5,110 away crowd at Bolton, the club and the fans were all over social media. County are news again and it feels great. Today though, is back to our bread and butter. The league and we have work to do. We are tenth, ten points behind top spot and five points off the play-off spots with a game in hand. The mood is that anything is possible under Challinor. He is the man for job. Bromley, however, are no mugs. They lie fourth, seven points ahead of us and the same games played. We know there will be no easy games.

Today was one of optimism and frustration. Two points dropped agonisingly in the last minutes. A clearance was pumped back into our box. The ball bounced around and was redirected towards our goal. With a Bromley forward behind him, Hogan somehow deflected the ball into the goal off his chest. It looked like another mistake by the unfortunate centre half. It was a nightmare ball played in front of him right on the goal line. Surely he could have hooked it away. To be fair, you had to sympathise with Hogan.

In the first half Quigley had put us ahead with a sublime finish. Taking the ball just outside the box, Scott dropped his shoulder, went past a defender and curled the ball low into the net. Quality finish and a touch of real class. County were much improved and this was our best performance all season to complement our much-improved cup performance against Bolton last week. The last-minute Hogan transgression aside, satisfaction replaced frustration quickly. We are desperate for the points but overall this was a decent point against a good Bromley side.

Live on TV under the lights showed what a great stadium Edgeley Park is at this level. It is a league standard ground. We need to get promoted. Swapping Rusk for Challinor has happened just in time. We trail the top two by ten points but with a game in hand. In his post-match interview, Dave Challinor said we need to put a run together. I have faith.

Wednesday 17th November 2021
FA Cup 1st Round Replay
County 5 Bolton 3 (after extra time)

An amazing effort by County fans has demonstrated the potential of this club. We sold out our tickets easily with Bolton also fulfilling their 1,300 allocation. The result is a sell-out 10,000-capacity crowd. For the last fifteen years the club has mostly been on a desperate decline. We've come back in the last few years and now we are living what only a few years ago would be described as a dream. Optimism, sell-out crowds and good football. Some progress was made under Rusk last season although entertainment was at a premium. Challinor has already added entertainment and attacking play.

On TV under the lights for consecutive matches, the excitement is palpable around the ground. Can we scrape it or will it be a thriller such as the 4-3 league win against the Trotters twenty years ago (when we were both plying our trade in the Championship). Again, the Cheadle End is in full voice. The national TV audience must be impressed. Dion Dublin and ex- County and Wales captain Ashley Williams are on the touchline near the Cheadle End. Both part of the BBC TV team. This is a big deal for us and a chance to remind the general public that County are alive and kicking.

County started well but within five minutes disaster struck twice. First a speculative shot is unluckily deflected past Ross off Kitching. Then Palmer got his feet in a tangle from a cross-shot and deflected into his own net. Two down after five minutes and the game was already drifting away. Fortunately, retribution for Palmer and Kitching was in the script. With the crowd behind them and a new spirit injected by Challinor, the team were not deterred. They just kept going. Bolton kept going too. A classic was already on the cards.

Midway through the half, Rydel cleverly held off a defender in the box and was fouled for a penalty. Duly dispatched by Madden, the Hatters were back in the game. Unbelievably, within five-minutes Bolton restored their two-goal advantage. It was another gift as Kitching headed past Ross and a Bolton forward raced on to the ball to convert easily. County were the better side but had gifted three goals to the opposition. Even with our generosity the feeling was we were still in the game. The crowd kept pushing the players on. A true twelfth man. The atmosphere was electric.

We scored at a perfect moment, just on the stroke of half time. Rydel crossed and Quigley rose to steer a classic angled header into the corner of the net.

The second half kicked off with County attacking the vociferous Cheadle End. The feeling was the home end would suck in an equaliser. County kept pressing. As the game went on we kept stretching Bolton but the Trotters looked a threat on the counter-attack. Eventually, with only five minutes to go, our bravery prevailed as Palmer headed in Rydel's in-swinging corner. Amazing scenes as the ground nearly exploded with elation. After gifting Bolton three goals, County dug deep to pull the game back to 3-3.

There was only one team in extra time. We wanted it more, the team wanted it more , the crowd wanted it more. The Bolton fans and their players were overcome by a wave of collective enthusiasm from Stockport. Genuine cup fever. In the first period of extra time we went ahead for the first time in the game. Madden's through ball into the box was lobbed over the keeper by the imperious Quigley. Even better was to come. In the last minute of the match, Crankshaw latched onto Raikhy's pass to slot home our fifth goal. The Cheadle End exploded again and a friendly pitch invasion ensued. With the pitch quickly cleared, the ref restarted the match and immediately blew for full-time.

The whole team and the subs were a collective spirit. A true team fighting for each other. Special mention goes to Quigley who looks a top striker. Southam-Hales was energy personified. Croasdale had grit, fight and determination. Crankshaw came on and was a menace down the wing. Raikhy defied youth with composure and quality highlighted by some sublime passes. Madden worked his socks off. Palmer and Kitching overcame the adversity of mistakes with powerful and determined performances. Special mention to new manager Challinor. Even at two down after five minutes, he looked composed, calm and controlled.

I superb match and atmosphere broadcast on TV to the country. One of the top ten matches ever at Edgeley Park. One to remember and cherish as new County legends were forged in an amazing come-back performance. The FA Cup is alive and kicking. County are alive and kicking. Challinor, after only three matches in charge, has invigorated the squad. There is every chance that we could put a successful promotion bid together now.

Tonight though was for the FA Cup and the reward is another visit to a League One club. This time to the New York Stadium. The strangely named South Yorkshire home of Rotherham United. Another clamour for tickets and another sold out away end. The County resurrection has started and the fans are on the rollercoaster. Proud of the team. Proud to be a Hatter tonight.

Saturday 20th November 2021
Woking 1 County 2

Buoyed by the magnificent cup endeavours of our heroic County, the Hatters faithful are back on the road down south to somewhere south-west of London. To Woking. Presumably one of those fairly dull London commuter towns. Or an even less attractively titled dormitory town. The literal meaning being a large bedroom. In this case a town catering for the massive magnet that is London. I am sure there are residents of good old Woking that never go to London. But the image is there. I have been to Woking before with work. I can recall duel carriageways and town centre by-passes and new buildings. Rather bland but there probably is a Woking olde town to be discovered.

Being a ground-spotter I checked out the Kingfield Stadium. But today will be my first actual visit in the ground for a match. I have to go to an exhibition near Glastonbury for work tomorrow, so there will be a diversion over to Dorset after the match. Then back home tomorrow night. More miles on the tachometer. Worth the while for two reasons. I still need to finance my bairns as they navigate through further education in the case of my two sons and starting a career in the case of my daughter.

Secondly, of course, to follow my football team. The latter taking a much improved and positive course over the last few exciting weeks. Only three matches into Challinor's reign but a very promising start. Great away cup draw at Bolton, very good performance against Bromley and heroic result a few days ago against Bolton in the FA Cup replay.

All this positivity aside, there is much work to be done in the league. For all the excitement of the cup, getting back to the football league is the priority. Challinor has said we need to put a run of wins together to climb the table. Maybe four victories out of the next five or similar. There is a gap that needs to be closed down. However, there are still thirty matches to play, so maybe there is plenty of time.

Hopefully, Wednesday's exertions hasn't taken too much fuel out of the players tanks. We have a big squad, so there is room for resting one or two players.

The trip down is an autopilot exercise. Saturday morning / early afternoon travel is much easier than mid-week mayhem as people commute and vehicles deliver. Some people literally get everything delivered from groceries to books to vapes. As people addictively order from the likes of Amazon, those delivery vans are going to breed like rabbits.

The journey via the M42 and M40 is one I've travelled numerous times. We used to go to Normandy on holiday regularly via the Portsmouth ferry. So this route is one where I know every service station and unfortunately every variable speed limit. Except this time I won't turn right towards Portsmouth, I'll carry straight on a collision course with southwest London.

Dropping off the M25, I navigated through some scenic Surrey forests and past the impressive entrance to the McClaren automotive headquarters. Once in the ground I join the other 300 Hatters loyalist on the terrace that runs the whole length of the pitch. Behind one goal is a large new looking stand that towers over the rest of the stadium. Behind the other goal is a small, covered terrace that houses their singers. Opposite us are two ramshackle seated stands.

Ben Hinchliffe replaces Ross for his 250th appearance for the club and has established himself as a club legend. Challinor may be resting Ross but Ethan has made a couple of mistakes recently letting Ben back in. The rest of the line-up is pretty much the same as the Bolton game and the team carried on where they left off. That being our new brand of faster, attacking play since the change in management.

Rusk's first match was at Woking which resulted in a 4-1 victory. One of a few highlights of his tenure. Even though Rusk managed an eighteen-match unbeaten run, it included a number of draws and victories against teams that had switched off towards the end of last season. Ultimately Rusk's style of play brought on his dismissal. Cagey, conservative and quite frankly boring. Challinor has transformed this team into positive, attacking and entertaining.

The slight worry today, is that the team are knackered after their extra time endeavours the other night. This wasn't evident as the players were full of vigour, controlling the game in the first half. After five minutes Madden swept home a Southam-Hales cross. Paddy doubled his tally on half an hour curling a nice shot into the top corner of the net. The Cardinals came back launching a few attacks but County controlled proceedings.

In the second half Woking stepped it up making a few chances before converting with twenty-five minutes left. Fatigue crept in but County worked hard as a team repelling late pressure. Southam-Hales was man of the match terrorising the Cards out wide. Madden was a contender with his brace of goals. We have now put a nice run together with winnable games at home to Kings Lynn on Tuesday and away to Wealdstone next Saturday.

At half time the Woking food van ran out of gas. With the search for another gas bottle proving a challenge I fortunately got the last pie. Chicken and mushroom. Decent too. The match was good and it was well worth the trip. Now for the hundred-mile journey across country to Dorset and work tomorrow.

Another ground visited as I attend matches around the country following County. This might be a special season. The omens look good and the three hundred kindred spirits at Woking today will agree.

Tuesday 23rd November 2021
County 5 Kings Lynn Town 0

Ole Gunnar Solskjaer has been sacked. I nice chap and United legend who unusually did an exit interview. An emotional video. He clearly loved the club. In a parallel thought I wondered what Rusk is doing. Do we care? The football manager is a short-lived role in the modern era. With the odd exception. Precarious but once sacked a well-compensated end. You need a thick skin as a manager, especially with social media. It got me thinking that football is all about fine margins.

There is a parallel between County and United. Both big spenders in their relative leagues assembling what should be title contending squads. Rusk navigated us to the play-off semi-finals last season. We lost to Hartlepool. Fine margins. Rusk didn't engender much love. His personality didn't give anything away. He was a closed book. His tactics were safe. A manager has to get a relationship going with supporters. If you can do that and entertain the fans, you have credit in the bank. Now we have Challinor and he ticks both boxes. There is a buzz around the club again.

Tonight we play the East Anglian Kings Lynn. They reside second bottom in the league. Only the points deducted desperate Dover are worse off. Kings Lynn went bust owing £77,000 in 2009 reforming as Lynn FC and now renamed Kings Lynn Town. That small amount of money is probably less than a day's pay for some Premier League stars. A club formed in 1881 went bust over a relatively paltry amount. It just highlights that there is something not quite right in football.

Supply and demand and the Premier League aside, the lack of distribution of cash seems at odds with the integrity of the game. The parachute payments received by teams relegated from the Premier League highlighting the unfair advantage teams gain. Whereby the likes of Fulham and Norwich will yo-yo between the Championship and the Prem. Whilst fallen giants such as Nottingham Forest, Sunderland and Sheffield Wednesday have an almost impossible task of regaining Premier League status.

Enough of that analysis, we're here for the National League. It's great to be a County fan again. The last few weeks have seen massive improvements and it feels as if we have a spirit and identity again. No more side-ball, back passing, containment and boring football. More passion, fight and attacking play. Simple really. Attack and score goals and the fans are happy. The potential of this squad is finally coming to the fore.

On a chilly Tuesday evening the first pinch of proper winter has kicked in. Multiple layers required in our Pop Side seats. The team soon warm us up with a top display. We looked like a team going for the title. Granted the opposition were lowly Lynn but we could have had seven or eight goals. County peppered their goal from the onset and only stoic defending repelled our shots. Kings Lynn held out until the breakthrough on the half hour as Keane volleyed into the top right corner. On half time the impressive Rydel blasted home a Croasdale through ball.

Within three minutes of the second half their keeper parried a shot from Quigley and man of the match Crankshaw headed home. Sub Barclay made it four with a half-volley from the edge of the box. With nine minutes left the introduction of substitute Connor Jennings was met with rapturous applause. Connor has been out for nine months recovering from a rare form of cancer which fortunately he has overcome. It must have been in the stars when the heroic Jennings scored our fifth in the last minute with a sweetly converted shot.

Our play was fast, positive and forward thinking. The team worked as a unit, constantly cajoling each other. Space was worked well creating constant options. Options turned into goal scoring opportunities. Opportunities resulted in five goals. We looked well drilled, well coached and well on our way to establishing a run of results that will propel us into the play-off spots.

The 32 Linnets supporters started to leave ten minutes before the end. Hats off to their loyalty and a long trip back to Norfolk. The 4,500 County fans were insulated from the cold with the glow of victory. Walking away from the ground everyone had a spring in their step. The chatter of voices had the tone of optimism. The mood within in the supporters is upbeat and the feeling is that we have a genuine title contending team. Looks like the play-offs are on the horizon with an outside chance of a title bid.

Next stop northwest London.

Saturday 27th November 2021
Wealdstone 1 County 4

Today we wheel our way to northwest London for a match with Wealdstone which is actually in Ruislip. I was a bit disingenuous to the area in the last book describing the sprawl of northwest London as scruffy and bland. I have worked there before. Last season I was incarcerated under lockdown and watched this match on the live streams. Today, I get to visit Ruislip and may have to eat my words in relation to the attractiveness of the surroundings.

Wealdstone are your archetypal non-league club. I expect a community club house and small terraces and stands. Their alumni includes hardmen Vinny Jones and Stuart Pearce. Also, "hardman" the Wealdstone Raider. The you tube celebrity a few years ago who offered out Whitehawk supporters and claimed they had no fans. A statement that can't be aimed at the 300 County fans expected today.

Last night I attended our annual industry awards event with work. This year it was in Birmingham. Conveniently on the way to Wealdstone. I knew I was travelling to the match today so the plan was to temper my alcohol intake. Even tempered, these occasions involve a late night and copious amounts of bonhomie. Slightly hungover, it would have been much easier to head north on a relatively relaxed journey back to Cheshire. However, there is a task in hand and I happily headed south instead.

With a full English breakfast inside me and a pint of coffee, the cobwebs of last night's excesses slowly subsided. Fortunately, the awards were in the hotel I was staying in so I didn't need to stumble through the streets of Brum. I managed to finish the night off in the hotel bar rather than take up offers of less than salubrious after-party destinations. My plans of tempering the alcohol intake predictably failed though!

Suitably in the right condition to drive, I pointed the German motor vehicle south. The trek down the M6 and M40 was rather uneventful. No major hold ups and within two hours I was in sunny Ruislip. Pronounced Rise-lip in them parts. At this point I will eat my words about northwest London. It is actually nice enough in Ruislip. Maybe I spent time in the less salubrious parts of the borough of Hillingdon in the past.

The Grosvenor Vale stadium is possibly taking the description of stadium a tad too far. It is very non-league. Barely National League level really. We are housed behind a goal in a pre-fab affair. A crinkly tin roof and what looks like transportable steps with seats on.

The back of the stand has no wall and let's an arctic wind whip through, up the back of my neck and infiltrates my five layers of clothing. I'm stood on the back row. It reminds me of the old Pop side at Edgeley Park when there was a big gap at the back letting wind whip through. It was snowing in Birmingham. It isn't here but it is colder.

The wind is wispy. The type that grabs hold of the ball in the air and changes it's direction. The play is a bit scrappy as passes go astray. I'm absolutely freezing, my hangover has returned and I'm 190 miles from home. Fortunately, the crowd is in good spirits. There are about twenty lads in fancy dress which makes me chuckle. I was starting to wonder why I wasn't nursing my hangover in the warmth of my own home when County scored. After half an hour Quigley continued his scoring run with a deflected shot from about twelve yards out. It warmed me up. Getting pangs of hunger I purchased a cheeseburger.

It was the worst burger I've ever had. The meat was lukewarm. Due to the freezing conditions, the bun and cheese were on their way to being frozen. Even the dying burger couldn't start to warm the cheese which was rock hard. To exacerbate the situation I had accidently squirted an excessive amount of freezing cold ketchup on it. After one and a half bites a carefully placed the remains on the ledge behind my back row seat. I don't think a famished fox or a desperate dog would touch it.

Fortunately, in the second half, Ollie Crankshaw scored an eighteen-minute hattrick. Ollie tapped in a cross after an hour then rifled home another four minutes later. On eighty minutes the hattrick was complete when our number 27 capitalised on a mistake and slotted the ball past the Stones keeper. Our hosts got a late consolation as Hinchliffe was beaten by a low shot from the edge of the box. We outclassed Wealdstone who were on a great run before this game. Their manager said they had been beaten by the Champions in waiting. County have been brilliant since Challinor took over and we now look like promotion candidates. Possibly Champions.

I jogged back to the car. Something I do at away games in the hope that I get a quicker escape. A bit of an advantage to beat some traffic. It probably doesn't make any difference. It provided an opportunity to warm up a bit. With my heated seat kicking in as I pulled away, I had already forgotten about my frozen first half doubts about making the journey. Another good County performance, another three points and another reason to be joyful.

By eight I was back up north and due at the Northenden Players social do. A karaoke night at a local theatre group that my wife is a member of. Some celebration pints to be had. No rest for the wicked!

CHAPTER FIVE
December 2021

Friday 3rd December 2021
(FA Cup 2nd Round)
Rotherham United 1 County 0

Cup runs bring out a wave of enthusiasm. At the Bolton home classic in the last round I had a couple of mates "What's Apping" from around the ground. Posting celebration videos with their kids who had requested to go to the game. Their Dad's aren't County fans. One was a Huddersfield fan the other a United fan. But they are local and their kids are going to school, talking about County and asking their Dad's to go to the match. Older lads such as our seventeen-year-old Jonnie are going with mates. I know at least two lads of a similar age who have got season tickets this season with a group of mates. What a refreshing change to everyone following City or United.

Tonight, we are going "en masse." A mate and our sons in a group of seven lads. Nine of us. All the lads are season ticket holders. Present and hopefully future loyal Hatters. We have an early excursion to take in the atmosphere, beat some of the Friday traffic and get some pre-match grub. Possibly a cheeky pint too. The lads should get served or we will arrange it. Jonnie looks about twenty-one anyway!

BBC news this morning had a decent feature on County and their cup exploits. Describing us as falling from the edge of the Premier League to regional part-time football. One of the most dramatic falls in the history of football. I believe it is the furthest any club have fallen apart from the ones that went bust. We are on the way back now though with a trip to table topping League One side Rotherham United.

In the last book I mentioned Rotherham as I passed their New York stadium with work. A sort of impressive edifice in the town centre. Across the duel carriageway from their old home Millmoor. The old ground is still there (I checked), slowly rotting away. Probably due to no one wanting to develop the site. If you have been, you will recollect it is hemmed in by scrap yards and factories. It was a dump when I went twenty odd years ago to watch County. But a good dump. In the sense it was an industrial, northern, ramshackle but characterful football ground. We will regret the creation of identikit, breeze block and cladding stadiums that look like retail units.

Today we transverse the picturesque Woodhead Pass, the scenic road that connects Greater Manchester to South Yorkshire. One of the few inter-city links that isn't a motorway. The civil engineering challenge required to tunnel a road through the moors and around the reservoirs proving too expensive or near impossible.

On arrival we partake in a quick pint in the Cutlers Arms a big pub with an impressive outside stage and marquee area. There are plenty of familiar faces from County mixing in with Millers fans. The stadium looks impressive if not a tad generic. A mixture of red and grey cladding which from some angles looks like a big Argos. The interior is better with staggered roof lines and two characterful spotlights leaning forward like something from War of the Worlds.

In the New York Stadium the 2,300 sell-out away end is in fine voice. Another pint was supped on the concourse as the teenagers in our party jostled around excitedly joining in the County hymns. We are on a fantastic run scoring goals for fun in the league and the FA Cup. There is a possibility that we are a match for the top of League One Millers. Possibility became reality as The Hatters dominated the first half. We had them on the back foot with a performance of spirit, energy and grit.

Crankshaw and Southam-Hales put the wind right up Rotherham. Constantly running and pushing their fullbacks. The only doubts were that once the Rotherham forwards got near our box their quick one-two passing looked dangerous. Without creating clear cut chances County looked impressive.

With our crowd providing the twelfth man effect though out the game, we continued the pressure in the second half. Madden had the ball in the net with a lovely stooping header but was just offside. The Millers decided that they didn't want to be embarrassed towards the end of the game and pulled their socks up. But it took a mistake by County just in front of our eighteen-yard box. A couple of loose passes gifting Rotherham possession before a quick as a flash passing combination was side footed past Hinchliffe. The quality I was worried about providing the winner for our hosts.

We have proven against Bolton and tonight that we are a match for League One sides. We have a number of players that have played at that level. It has taken eighteen months since Stott took over to get to this point. A false dawn under Rusk and now the real deal with Challinor.

County and our fans produced a magnificent effort. It was great to be with a group of teenagers singing proudly and enjoying a big away match. These games make County fans. Nobody was disappointed as we put up a great show. We can now concentrate on the league. Even the most cautious Hatters fan will feel confident that we can get promoted.

The Millers manager said that County matched them. He said the County fans were the best he'd ever seen at the New York Stadium. Good enough for me.

Tuesday 7th December 2021
Cheshire Senior Cup
Macclesfield 1 County 3

We can now concentrate on the league but we are still in two cups. The FA Trophy with a home draw against Grimsby. Plus the Cheshire Senior Cup, our fixture this evening. Many County fans discount this as unimportant. But when you are at a certain level, you are in certain competitions. Some fans even think that attendance of such matches are for the eccentrics or egg butty fans. I think the egg butty reference is for the ones that go all the way to places like Weymouth on a coach with a packed lunch in a rucksack etc. I suppose I kind of qualify.

Tonight is an easy thirty minutes down the A34 from my house for a Cheshire derby. Being a footy nutter/ eccentric I am looking forward to this one. It is probably fifteen years since I've been to the Moss Rose. It is a traditional type ground. Macc Town went bust just before the pandemic and have become a phoenix club renamed Macclesfield FC. Plying their trade at local non-league level, they are top of their league riding a wave of optimism. Local resident Robbie Savage is involved and a documentary is on TV telling their story. Crowds have doubled even though they are way down the pyramid.

Tonight will be an opportunity to see some fringe players. We have a big squad and Challinor will be assessing the future. I am sure he is thinking about next season already. What if we get back into the League? Who do I keep, what do I need etc? We are perfectly equipped to get out of this league and survive in League Two. Nothing is guaranteed but the management team will have a strategy in place. We've come a long way in a short space of time since the reign of Rusk. Rusk was ok but you never thought there was a masterplan. It was like stumbling along in the general direction of the play-offs. Rather than the current performances whereby we look like we deserve to win the league.

Tonight is the cup though. I don't even know how many rounds there are or where the final is. That level of info must be for the egg butty brigade! Full respect to them. I'll google it. There are 25 teams in it. It started in 1880 and the final is at a neutral ground. We of course won it in 15/16 beating Tranmere 2-1 at Nantwich. That was in the middle of our dark days.

Macc have won this trophy more times than anyone else. You would think they are taking it seriously. I'm taking this seriously. So seriously I'm making the trip feeling a bit rough. I had my booster shot yesterday and I'm aching all over. No reaction on the first two Astra Zeneca but the booster was Moderna. I'm feeling a bit like an advocate turned into a skeptic. Surely my good old immune system has built up enough antibodies. Best to follow the advice though.

The weather is shocking. Pelting it down. About as damp as meteorologically possible. I'm stood with the nutters in the rain on the terrace behind the goal. Originally the tickets were in covered seats but the allocation was sold and they've moved us onto the open terrace. The wind is swirly and freezing. By the second half the rain returns. The phrase pissed wet through being the perfect description for our predicament.

The pitch is 4G which helps. It is wet but at least it won't be a mud bath. I'm prepared. Five layers of clothing. Waterproof shoes and coat. Thick socks. Woolly hat. Wise owl. I can see youngsters with County shirts and jackets, trainers and nothing on their head.

The ball is delivered to the centre spot by a remote-control jeep. From distance it looks like a Tonka toy. The ball is then removed by the ref before the vehicle U-turns and speeds off. I've seen it in the Bundesliga and possibly the Champions League. The Cheshire Senior Cup is cutting edge!

County jog on in all yellow. A kit that isn't one of our first team kits this season but has been used by the academy. The line-up is completely changed. Tom Walker, Connor Jennings and Raikhy are in complimented by squad players Pye, Earl and Alli. Once the whistle blows I warm up a bit. On twenty minutes Jennings scores to put us ahead before Macc equalise within five minutes from the penalty spot. On half time the impressive Alli drove a nice, angled shot from the edge of the box into the corner of the net.

County dominated the second half before scoring a third on the hour. Academy player Edwards making his family proud by scoring for the senior team. The wind kept swirling. Two more academy players came on. Nock and Tanswell getting an opportunity to impress. An impressive 1,054 braved the elements. Great turnout for a low-key fixture in Baltic conditions.

All the excitement had warmed me up no end. I jogged to the car. A couple of layers were discarded. The heated seat was switched on and I whisked my way down the A34 with a glow of victory. We are into the quarter-finals. Worth the trip. Who says the Cheshire Senior Cup isn't important.

Saturday 11th December 2021
Torquay United 2 County 1

I'll miss one or two away matches such as Dover. This is another one where I'll tune into Strawberry radio and our excellent match commentator Jon Keighren. I'm not sure if the station has any connection to Strawberry Studio's a famous Stockport recording studio. I'm used to twiddling the knobs of radio myself being an amateur rock presenter. Metaphorically speaking of course as there are no knobs these days. It is all copy and paste MP3 files. But back in the heyday of Strawberry Studios, many a famous artist twiddled the knobs of the mixing desk.

Most famous being the Stockport band 10cc. Strawberry Studios was their home studio used to record their hits. They had a few. Five consecutive top ten albums. One of the biggest bands in the world and undoubtably Stockport's biggest ever group. Two members; Lol Creme and Kevin Godley went on to become some of the most sort after producers. Most notably, the duo went on to become A list music video producers. Pretty much every top artist collaborated with the Stopfordians.

Always nice to muse over Stockport history but of course this book is focussed on the towns football team. They are doing just fine at the moment. Another reason to listen on the radio is that I've promised to go to a pub gig my wife is doing tonight. Kath is in the Interns a covers band. Good stuff too. So the impossible task of getting back from Devon in time requires radio tuneage today. My attendance of the Cheshire Cup match at Macc the other night providing peace of mind that I had fulfilled County duty this week.

I've been to Plainmoor once before as regaled in my previous book. In August 1977. Elvis died while we were there. I was on holiday with my grandparents and we went to an early season match. The main recollection being skinheads scrapping. Possibly unrelated to the match itself;

a 1-0 League Cup win for the Gulls versus the Bluebirds of Cardiff. I say unrelated as we were neutral holidaymakers so the aggro could have been other vacationers. My brother and Grandad went.

Our next aggro watching occurred a few years later as neutrals again watching Oldham v Chelsea in the old Second Division. At a perishing Ice Station Zebra (Boundary Park) we evaded missiles from the Londoners in the seats above us. The "Oldhamers" responded with a charge towards the Chelsea "fans" that jumped into our paddock. All a bit scary for us young uns but the local constabulary soon repelled the southern hordes back into their seats.

In less risky times the Hatters visit the Gulls for a National League encounter this afternoon. I will listen to it all on Strawberry radio. I am allergic to shopping, so there is no chance of seeing me milling around a shopping centre even if it is Xmas soon. I get all my clothes as seasonal gifts and the only physical retail shopping I do is to enter HMV to check out the CD's and the resurrected sales of vinyl. Typical bloke you may opine but I made this quite clear to my lovely wife at the very start of our relationship. I like football, music and drinking beer and that is unlikely to change until I pop my clogs. Of course compromise occurred as I learnt to cook and do a variety of DIY.

Disappointment down in Devon is the strap line for this game. After a run of great performances the lads ran out of steam. Quigley out ill meant we went with Madden and Crankshaw up front requiring a change in tactics. On the ground footy without the big man up front option. Truth be told the team as a whole had an off day. A reality check that the season is a long haul. 260 loyalists made the journey. In hindsight I'm glad I didn't. Five hours each way deserves a service medal for all the Hatters in attendance.

County made a rare appearance in their white shirts / black shorts away kit (we've used the pink third kit a lot this season). In damp and gloomy conditions County started brightly. We had more chances but failed to convert. The play was laboured compared to our recent quick and incisive style. The Gulls scored first as Collar deflected a shot that was going wide into his own net. Will immediately made amends with the equaliser. A header from a Rydel cross straight from the re-start.

County shot themselves in the foot again by conceding a soft penalty. Sarcevic needlessly barging a player down in the box. Reid came on near the end providing Alex another chance to shine. He didn't which means Challinor will have made the decision that we need an alternative striker.

The Hatters had multiple chances, more than the Gulls. To no avail. We were our own worst enemy with the pen and an own goal. That's football. But we need to ensure any further defeats are kept to a minimum to stay in the hunt for top spot.

Saturday 18th December 2021
FA Trophy
County 4 Grimsby Town 0

Just when we thought we could concentrate on the league, today is another cup match. Knocked out of the FA Cup I almost forgot about the Cheshire Senior Cup. Then I had to remind myself that we have today's game in the FA Trophy. This is the non-league version of the FA Cup with the final at Wembley. The entrants are from Step 1 of non-league (us) to step 4. A match at Wembley makes it worthwhile for probably half of our fans. Half just want to concentrate on the league. I fall into the let's win it half and get a trip to the citadel of English football.

The defeat at Torquay has slightly tempered our recent super-enthusiasm. I'm sure Challinor will have addressed anything in training this week. The Gulls have a good home record but we were off colour. You can understand a drop in energy after our recent scoring run and exploits against League One sides. We have a chance to get back on track this afternoon against the Mariners.

For today's game we are having a change again by buying seats in the Main Stand. Our usual Pop Side seats are good but it's nice to have a change of view. I've spent most of my County life watching in the Cheadle End but prefer a side on view in the Pop Side these days. A benefit of the Pop Side is you can just walk straight in even close to kick-off rather than queue up for the Cheadle End. Plus they now sell beer and you get served quickly rather than the melee that exists for drinks down inside the Cheadle End.

Taking our seats in the centre of the Main Stand, I have to say this is the best view in the house. Contrary to what some people think it's not full of old blokes either. I like the fact you are close to the benches too and can watch the managers prowling around the technical areas.

The Mariners suffered a home defeat to top of the league Chesterfield on Saturday. They are in a similar league position to us so this should be a close match. However, we have been transformed recently under our new manager so are clear favourites with home advantage today.

Challinor picked a strong team demonstrating that the boss is taking this cup seriously. A few were rested but the line-up is one that could be picked for a league match. County dominated. Sat near the technical areas, we got a full show of their managers frustrations as we put his team to the sword. To be fair, it looked like they fielded a few youngsters. However, we bossed proceedings from start to finish.

Man of the match Will Collar bagged two. His impressive midfield mate Croasdale pitched in and the scoring was completed by the consistent Ash Palmer. Another impressive performance. Also impressive was the culinary fair. County employed new caterers last season. The pies are top notch. Today I partook in the double cheeseburger. A beast of a thing which was tasty and took me a good fifteen minutes to devour. Great footy and grub. Life is good.

We have drawn Larkhall Athletic in the next round at home. They ply their trade in the Southern League and are based near Bath. The Larks are in step four of non-league. A big day out at Edgeley Park for them.

Sunday 26th December 2021
County 5 Altrincham 1

It's the traditional Boxing Day local derby against our Cheshire rivals Altrincham. My family is up in the Lakes in a hired house for a festive break for a week. That includes three brother in laws, their wives, kids, mother-in-law and our kids. Walks, games, food and beverages. The usual Chrimbo excesses. My daughter who now lives and works in London is coming back to Manchester to see other relatives. So I'll be nipping back for the Alty match and driving her up to the Lakes to share in our seasonal bonhomie.

What do we want for Christmas? Three points of course.

We are wearing our white away shirts with black shorts today. This is for the Shelter charity no home kit campaign. County historians will know that this was our home kit from the early thirties to mid-sixties. But you'd have to be pretty old to remember it in the flesh. It is a smart kit but I'm so used to blue that it seems strange to see our boys at home in different colours.

Alty are sporting yellow shirts. As a traditionalist, I'd prefer both teams to don their home kits. But it is for a good charity today. The Main Stand and Cheadle End are sold out. The Pop side is nearly full. Great effort by the fans. The crowd of just under 9,000 is our biggest home league match attendance since 2008. There is a Xmas buzz and many are sporting seasonal hats and jumpers. There is a footy buzz amongst the County hordes as we are on the up, scoring goals and looking like title challengers. You can't beat a Boxing Day derby.

In a barnstorming opening fifteen minutes, The Hatters scored three and could have had more. The 740 Alty fans were knocked for six. It should have been more but we "only" got five in the end. Sarcevic, Madden, Quigley and Will Collar scored four first half goals with Croasdale scoring an own goal for our visitors. 4-1 at half time. Alty were outclassed. Pick of the first half goals was Collars drilled shot from a Southam-Hales cross.

In the second half, Alty put up a much better fight, holding a better shape to thwart County. We kept creating chances though and could have had another three goals. Only one was bagged but it was the best of the match. Collar played a one-two with Crankshaw, who volleyed home from a tight angle to make it five and send more than 8,000 County fans wild with festive joy.

Awesome stuff. The Hatters were in full flow, full of running and goal threat. We are scoring freely and outplaying teams. Many of the players have improved or hit form. But the best signing of 2021 must be manager Dave Challinor. Since DC arrived, these players have fulfilled their potential. I'll be having more festive beers tonight before returning to the Lakes tomorrow with my daughter. Then more festive celebrations are guaranteed. With County in this form I'm doubly buzzing at the moment.

Here's looking forward to Solihull away and then a very optimistic 2022 for the Super Hatters!

Tuesday 28th December 2021
Solihull 0 County 1

I nipped back for the Alty match and have brought Daniela back to the Lakes. Nipping down to Solihull and back is tricky. Plus it would use up most of the time I have to be with Daniela. Football is a priority for me but you can only take it so far. Never mind, hopefully I'll never get the chance to watch a match at Solihull. The priority for County is to go up and presumably avoid another visit to the Moors. Having said that, our opponents are doing well. They are in fact above us in the league table.

In a repeat of the Alty match, County are in the white away shirts and Solihull in an almost exact replica of Alty. Moors sport yellow shirts and blue shorts, the same as the Alty away kit. Strawberry Radio provided the description until I saw the highlights. I managed to put a couple of hours of time aside to listen to the commentary. We are buried away in the Langdale hills near Ambleside where there is radio silence. Fortunately, I have the Strawberry Radio app and wi-fi connection. Jon Keighren our intrepid commentator is coming through loud and clear in Lakeland. We dominate the first half against a very good Moors side who have registered several clean sheets recently. 0-0 at the break. This isn't going to be easy.

There is an expectation now that we are going to win every match. That isn't possible and there will be points dropped. Confidence is at an all-time high so as the game progresses in the second half, there is frustration that we haven't scored. A point away at Solihull is a decent result but would be tinged with disappointment due to our current excellent form. We are pressing and creating chances and Madden in particular sounds like he's getting in the right positions before being thwarted by last ditch blocks.

In the second half, both teams hit the bar and Quigley has a few chances. With twenty minutes to go it sounded like it may be one of those days when nothing goes in. Relief soon came with seventeen minutes left. Collar's deep cross from the right found Madden beyond the far post and the striker's header looped over the Moors goalie to put County ahead. Right in front of the sold out away end. Watching the highlights the conversion was a classic slow looper, perfectly executed by the excellent Madden.

Another victory that takes us into sixth place just four points from second. Seven points from table topping Chesterfield. We play the Spireites on Feb 8th at home with an opportunity to narrow that gap. The chase is on. The Hatters are ready to hunt down top spot. Back to the Lakeland festive celebrations for now. Back to the footy soon. 2021 closes on a very upbeat note.

CHAPTER SIX
January 2022

Tuesday 11th January 2022
Altrincham 1 County 4

Today was scheduled as the traditional festive return fixture versus our local rivals. It was postponed and re-arranged due to covid in the Alty ranks. This is the first fixture I looked for at the at the start of the season. A proper local derby in a proper old ground.

I missed the first batch of tickets in the pre-Xmas rush. With short notice, season ticket holders had one day to get them which I missed. When a balance of about 300 extra tickets went on open sale, I missed out again. I had just descended a hill in the Lakes. Soaking wet through we got in a café in Grasmere just on 12pm when they went on sale. On my phone, I chased seats around the seating plan like a game of Pac-Man. I eventually caught two and went all the way through the payment section before being told the tickets had gone.

Fortunately, Alty still had plenty on sale in the home end. On returning from the Lakes, I nipped down to Moss Lane and bought two tickets no problem. Despite warnings that the tickets weren't for away fans and proof of address was required, the friendly chap asked no questions. I must look like an Alty type of fan. Or smile in a convincing manner. It was all a bit premature as the match was postponed due to the covid cases. Today is the re-arranged match that should have been played on the 3rd January.

Alty are my favourite other team in non-league. My Grandad was from the town before moving to Stockport. Although a big United fan, he took me and my brother to Moss Lane to watch The Robins on several occasions. They have loyal support with a great variation of songs. The ground is a classic old school affair. They suffer from being a town full of United and City fans (even more than us). Alty were denied entry into the football league on several occasions and could be described as unlucky.

I'm with eldest son Will who's back from Uni and we are undercover tonight as we have tickets in the Alty areas. We take our spot on the halfway line opposite the main stand on the Pop Side terrace. To our right is the Golf Road terrace where the home sides vocal fans reside when Alty are kicking that way. In a non-league tradition the home singers move over to the Pop side when kicking the other way. To the left of us is the Chequers End where the County fans are stood. Anyone old enough will remember this terrace is named after the long-lost night club that lay just behind the terrace and is now a block of flats.

The main stand has two new-ish buildings either side. A small, seated family stand which houses County fans tonight and a new community centre on the other side. This centre includes a big, impressive bar.

There is temporary fencing around the back of the Golf Road and Pop Side corner. Alty have had reduced capacity this season due to some non-compliance of pitch boundary walls and general disrepair of bits of the ground. No surprise to me. From the main road Moss Lane looks neat. But go around the back of the Pop Side or Golf Road and the stands are a mixture of old corrugated iron and ancient concrete. They haven't been upgraded for forty plus years. Hopefully, their National League status will bring in the extra revenue required to spruce up the old place.

Pre-match we got a free pint from my sons mate who's working behind the Alty bar. A number of County fans are guided into the away end past us. We stay in with the Alty fans as we can go back into the bar for another subsidised pint at half time. The ground is packed. 3,900 with 1,500 Hatters supporters. Returning to tradition, both teams are in their home kits after the no home kits charity Boxing Day match up. County have a slight change with the introduction of blue socks.

Will rarely see's County these days and his conclusion during the first half was that County are quality and to expect a 4 or 5-0. It was 2-0 at half time. Alty to be fair played their part but our speed of passing and movement was faster than our hosts. After only six minutes Sarcevic converted from six yards. Just before half time we scored a goal of pure class. Some nice interplay fell to Collar who blasted a straight powerful shot into the top right-hand corner of the goal from twenty-five yards.

At the start of the second half, Madden converted a penalty to effectively finish Alty off. Our opponents kept plugging away but our superiority was clear to see. Just after the hour Croasdale scored a header for 4-0. I was ok with Altrincham scoring a consolation goal in the last minute. The Alty fans are a good bunch and they celebrated around us. There was some nice banter with the County fans near us which was a bit strange being in with the home fans. Dave Challinor went over to the fans at the end high fiving the happy Hatters.

The mist settled on Moss Lane with steam rising from the players under floodlights on a classic winter away day scene. This County side look like they are going to relentlessly hunt down the teams above them in the table. The other teams above us who played all won tonight. However, now we are fulfilling our potential, there is every chance we can threaten top spot and a play-off place looks a certainty.

Saturday 15th January 2022
FA Trophy
County 3 Larkhall Athletic 0

Last Saturday's home league game v Chesterfield didn't happen as the Spireites were still in the FA Cup. It provided an un-scheduled winter break for the players. Fortunately the Alty away match was quickly re-arranged for Tuesday.

Patience is something County fans are used to. After the 2008 Wembley play off final and promotion to League 1, the last twelve or so years have been mostly a disaster. The last few have seen recovery but subsequent years after 2008 were one disappointment after another. We hit the nadir of relegation from League 2. Then that nadir was usurped by the ultimate nadir of relegation to regional non-league football and the drop into the National League North. It was the furthest a team had ever fallen. Apart from clubs that went bust. From finishing eighth in what is now the Championship, we tumbled down five leagues.

Each pre-season the fans believed recovery would occur. Reality was that the club had financially imploded. Dodgy consortiums came and went. Skint and with no real professional management, the club relied on volunteers and fan management. Somehow we didn't go bust and green shoots of recovery started to appear. Unbelievably we spent four seasons in the National League North. 2018/19 eventually saw us promoted back into the National League. Faith was restored. The Mark Stott takeover has been revolutionary. What a year 2021 has been.

I am looking forward to today's match against Larkhall, a team in the fourth tier of non-league football. The FA trophy is the FA Cup of non-league with the final at Wembley. This is the equivalent of a Premier League side playing a League 2 side. A massive match in the history of Larkhall Athletic founded in 1914. They ply their trade in the Southern League Division 1. The Larks are based near Bath. Their ground capacity is 1,000. This is a football dream for Larkhall. As a footy nut, this match has all the romance of the cup.

I'm in my "cup seat" in the Main Stand. I switch from the Pop Side for cup matches to get a different view. My thoughts drift to potential matches. In 2021 we held our own against West Ham, Bolton and Rotherham. Amazing performances. Today we play Larkhall. In the next few years it could be back to Portsmouth, Sunderland or Sheffield Wednesday. League 1 is a possibility. A realistic target. Today though is for the cup.

The Larks have brought about 170 fans. Not bad considering they average 150. The overall crowd is an impressive 3,500, the highest of the day in the FA Trophy. Victory will take us into the last sixteen with Wembley as the final destination. The day is crisp with perfect blue skies. There are ten changes but nine replacements are what could be considered first teamers such is the depth of our squad. The exception is academy captain Scott Holding who partners Jordan Keane in defence. Scott was my man of the match with a mature display and no errors. The sponsors chose Connor Jennings who scored twice.

Connor got his brace in a first half totally dominated by the Hatters. We should have had four at least. That would have been a bit unfair to our plucky but physical visitors. Three divisions difference showed. Tom Walker in particular came in for a bit of treatment. Tom's quality took him past defenders and they had to foul him several times to stop the threat. Unfortunately for Tom, I don't think he did enough to impress Challinor into re-introducing him into the first team. Another disappointment was Alex Reid. Nice and tidy but no real threat to a defence from several levels below us.

In the second half, academy player Josh Edward's came on for Kitching and looked solid. Home debutant Ryan Johnson scored to complete a comfortable 3-0 victory. The Larks got warm applause from the home fans before and after and for their substitutes. This was one of the biggest games in their history. They get half the gate receipts which is around £15,000. That is approximately a year's budget and is a massive financial boost for them.

It is great to be a Hatters fan at the moment. Apparently we are the highest scorers in all of football in the last few months along with Man City and Fulham. Games are coming fast now with a Saturday/Tuesday schedule. Next up the Spitfires from Eastleigh.

Tuesday 18th January 2022
County 3   Eastleigh 0

Eastleigh is near Southampton and they are nicknamed the Spitfires. The first Spitfire was built in Southampton and first flown from Eastleigh Aerodrome, now Southampton Airport. They were formed in 1946 and played regional non-league until about twenty-five years ago before rising up the pyramid. Their Spitfire name was chosen in 2005 through a fan competition. They are now a mid-table National League team. It has been good to play all the new teams as we went up and down the leagues. But no disrespect to Eastleigh, we do need to get back to the Football League and return to playing more traditional league teams.

Tonight Jonnie joins me on the Pop Side, back in our season ticket seats. He's missed a few matches recently as he works in a restaurant part time in combination with being a sixth former. Eldest son Will has returned to Uni after watching a couple of matches. I love taking my lads. There's nothing better than sharing the experience and having the banter. Now we share a beer too. I'm still buying but hopefully the further education will pay-off and they will keep me in beer soon. It is decidedly nippy tonight with the thermometer just above freezing.

On the back of the TV gantry near our seats there has always been a sign requesting no swearing. Profanity in this part of the Popside has reduced significantly in recent years. It is a joy to attend now. Thank God the team have improved and I can easily recruit my lads. There were several years when the only reason I sat here on a cold Tuesday night was through blind loyalty. Now it is for the entertainment as well. We need to savour these days. The team are delivering in spades now.

Today was another fairly routine win even though Eastleigh put up a fair fight. There are few easy games in this league. All the teams are physical and fit. Even the part time sides are athletic and keep going to the end. Occasionally our full-time training pays off in the last ten minutes but this league is effectively the same level of fitness and skill as League 2 in the EFL.

In the first half Scott Quigley was just about to head in when a defender did Scott's job for him and headed into his own net. Followed by another fortuitous goal when Madden scuffed a shot that deflected off a defender into the goal. Technically an o.g. but credited to Paddy. The second half saw Eastleigh loanee Maghoma pick up a quick-fire brace of yellow cards reducing our visitors to ten men. County peppered the visitors goal hitting the woodwork more than once before Jennings sealed the victory with a shot just inside the box.

My five layers insulated me from the freezing temperatures. County were red hot again on the pitch. Another victory on what is becoming a march on top spot that looks like giving us a chance at winning the league. Before DC became manager we were sixteen points behind the leaders. In a quick-fire run of results, the team are within touching distance of the summit.

Saturday 22nd January 2022
Dagenham & Redbridge 0 County 2

Best laid plans are scuppered by the TV schedulers today. BT are taking the mickey in a similar vein to the inconsideration shown by TV companies to Premier League fans. Today is a 5:20pm kick-off. If you want to catch the Fingerpost Flyer coach, it leaves Stocky at 10am and returns around 1am. A 3pm kick off would have been far more convenient. Good job someone reminded me of the kick-off time. I nearly booked a hotel.

The plan was to combine the match with a visit to see my daughter on her birthday. Daniela resides near the Oval cricket ground now she works in London. If it was a 3pm match, I could have nipped across from East London for a meal and drinks etc. With it being more like 9pm before a possible London rendezvous it cramps our style. I'll save it for the several other London visits still in our away match schedule.

It will be a nice novelty to see County on the telly. I have BT Sport so no problem tuning in from the comfort of my sofa with a beer. We've been on the box several times this season due to our cup exploits and TV league matches. I've been at all the televised games so this will be a TV debut for me. In a change from our historical bad results when on TV, recently we have been great in front of the camera's. Fingers crossed that continues.

As mentioned in the last book, I've been to Victoria Road (or the blandly renamed Chigwell Construction Stadium) before. Dagenham is bang in the middle of the East London sprawl. Not the most picturesque location. The ground is surrounded by industrial units. Plumbing and car part outlets etc. The County faithful are housed behind the goal in the largest, seated stand. This is a big match as The Daggers are fellow promotion candidates. In fact they are all big matches now. But today is a tough challenge. They are near the top of the form table.

On the box it seems strange to see our travelling fans and not being there. I've listened to a couple of matches on the radio but this is the first time I've seen the super Hatters on telly this season. There is a decent turnout of about 350 which is good considering the kick-off time and the TV appearance. You can hear them loud and clear. When your team is doing well there is an extra tunefulness about the chants. A confidence.

It didn't need much extra to motivate our away support. But they got it. The first five minutes of this match was a tsunami. The Daggers didn't know what hit them. It must have been like playing Barcelona or even City (as much as I don't like mentioning them). County were relentless. Pressing and bullying the home side into submission. If a match could be won in the first five minutes then this was that match.

After just three minutes Palmer rose in his classic style to plant a header from a Rydel cross into the Daggers net. Two minutes later Collar converted his sixth goal in seven matches. A cross was driven into the box with Collar the quickest to react running on to the ball to force it past the Dagenham keeper. County's high pressing game caused all sorts of problems for the hosts. The Daggers manager wondered what hat hit them. In the second half he made a triple change to try to inject some reaction. This backfired when within moments, defender Elliot Johnson fell to the turf injured. No more subs allowed. With only ten men the game was up for our hosts and fellow promotion challengers. County professionally saw the game out with little threat on our goal.

In what was considered a very tough test against an in-form side, County passed with flying colours. One of the most impressive performances so far. We looked like champions. There is still work to do but a challenge for the title is on. A play-off spot looks likely. Now, after a series of top-notch performances and victories, we look like the best side in the league.

Tuesday 25th January 2022
County 3   Maidenhead United 0

A consecutive Tuesday night home match sees County under the lights poised for a move to the summit of the league table. If we win tonight we go top for the first time this season. Similar to last Tuesday against Eastleigh the temperature is hovering just above freezing as I continue with five layers of clothing. This season I've introduced a woolly hat and gloves. Even though I'm a biker that up until recently went out in all-weather all year round, I have moved into a built for comfort mode. Jonnie meanwhile is a typical teenager who seems to have polar bear like resistance.

Tonight, for some reason, the Cheadle End drummer and his mates have decided on the Pop Side. After an initial left of centre position they move to the centre to join the Pop Side singers. I wonder what the regulars think of the youthful invasion. The drummer bangs out a rhythm. The two sets of singers soon synchronise. Not sure why they've moved or whether it is permanent. Possibly something to do with some newer youths in the Cheadle End who have been acting up. Anyway, a welcome addition if they fancy staying.

Maidenhead or the Magpies as they are known (their home kit is black and white), are our next challenge. They enter the field in their yellow and green away kit looking like Norwich. They are massive. To a man they all look over six foot. I was at the away fixture and didn't notice that they were particularly imposing. They are also in form. They have beaten our fellow title challengers Halifax and Chesterfield in their last two games. After about five minutes a realise they are also very good.

In fact, Maidenhead look like one of the best teams we have played this season. Their manager and ex- West Ham legend Alan Devonshire has them well drilled. Strong, organised and athletic. They keep their shape at all times. The first half is frustrating. Our opponents have made us look average. We have been excellent at pressing teams but Maidenhead have such a good shape, that it's difficult to get past them. The closest anyone comes to scoring is Maidenhead as we have to put in a couple of last-ditch interceptions to thwart them.

Half time allowed Challinor to work his magic. County came out with an extra zip which started to unlock the Magpie's defence. Within twenty seconds Madden smashed our first chance of the match just over. Invigorated we had Maidenhead on the back foot. But we encountered stubborn resistance and they looked a threat on the break. However, County were in the ascendency. Eight minutes into the second half, Sarcevic converted a looping header. It was greeted with possibly the loudest roar of the season. There was some relief in that roar.

Ollie Crankshaw came on and made a difference. His speed causing problems for the Magpie's. Ollie worked a ball into Sarcevic who fed Croasdale and his drilled shot nestled in the back of the net. The visitors were still a threat with Hogan and Southam-Hales making last ditch blocks. Rooney came on and in injury time drilled a shot into the top left-hand corner of Maidenhead's net. Edgeley Park erupted. Tricky first half but all ended up well with a much improved second half performance.

We had a first opportunity of the season to sing "we are top of the league." This was complimented with renditions of various "going up" songs. That is eight wins in a row. We are not going to win every game but if we carry on like this we have a great chance of winning the division.

Saturday 29th January 2022
Barnet 0   County 5

In a season of mostly long distance away matches you get used to the miles. I suppose it's a bit like being a Plymouth fan whereby every opponent is north. The famous maritime city is not only extremely south, but also extremely west. With the exception of the odd Devon derby, all their away games are miles away. London is 200 miles, Birmingham 210, Manchester 280 and Newcastle an eye watering 410 miles.

Barnet therefore is just a hop skip and a jump for me today. In fact it feels like an easy one. Just at the end of the M1. So no need to go around the M25 or mess about going through various towns. Just an exit off the motorway on the edge of north London. Easier than the various south coast and south London destinations this season.

After my aborted attempt to see Daniela on her birthday (Dagenham away on the 22nd January), today will be the day. The Daggers meet up was aborted as BT Sports inconsiderately decided on a 5:20pm kick off. It's a 3pm kick off today, hotel is booked with an easy train into the big smoke afterwards. I have the company of my wife Kath too.

Barnet's ground is neat but uninspiring. The Bee's call it The Hive. Except there isn't much activity in their hive as they only get an average 1,500 fans. That will be boosted today by the hordes of Hatters. Or the 700 or so County fans that will boost the crowd to over 2,000. The Hive is part of a sports complex. The Spurs ladies and London Bee's ladies play there. It is functional and tidy I suppose. But not really a dedicated football ground. Barnet's old ground, Underhill, was ramshackle but it was theirs. I'm glad that County plan to develop Edgeley Park and retain its character.

After a trouble-free journey we parked at the ground. The tariff of eight quid feeling like London weighting. However, fifty-three quid for an Ibis hotel softened the blow. We got a quick look at Crystal Palace v Barnet ladies on one of the Astroturf pitches. There is a large bar at the back of the away end which is quite impressive. The County choir were in fine tune. Entering the ground we have three blocks with around 780 County fans. Fantastic following for a London match. The recent form boosting the numbers as we hit top spot in the league.

The attendance was declared as 2,300. It looks like we have as many fans as them so the split looks debatable. The Bees have dire crowds. Apparently part of the reason is that we are not actually in Barnet. We are in neighbouring Edgeware. According to home fans, Barnet Council screwed them on planning permission to develop the site of their old ground at Underhill. To add insult to injury a rugby club from outside the borough were given permission to build their new ground in Barnet.

On the pitch County were countered by a swirling wind and industrial tackling from the giants of Barnet. Another imposing line-up of physical hackers looking like a combination of heavy weight boxers and basketball players.

The ref was lenient. Reminiscent of 1970's football. Their players had a free hit on our lads before consideration for a yellow card.

Early on, there was a five-minute stoppage on the far side for no apparent reason. Later we learnt that County defender Ryan Johnson was allegedly racially abused by a member of Barnet's staff. Ryan got some justice by scoring two goals. Controversially, Barnet tried to sweep the incident under the carpet resulting in their captain and a number of players threatening to go on strike. Shockingly Barnet then threatened to sack them. The Bee's saw sense and retracted their threat and admitted to the incident. Disgraceful behaviour by Barnet and an illustration of the work still needed to be done to eradicate racism in society.

We didn't really get going until half an hour had past and the swirling wind subsided. After several shots on goal we scored on half time. It was difficult to make out who headed home from our position at the other end of the pitch. It was the in-form Will Collar for an impressive seven goals in nine games.

After the break County kept it on the floor more and dominated play. Four more goals were scored. Rydel got another assist as Johnson headed in. Rydel repeated his set piece mastery. This time Hogan obliged with his header. Liam then celebrated extatically in front of the Hatters faithful. Hogan is back in form and there was relief as well as ecstasy. John Rooney's quickly taken free-kick found Connor Jennings, who drilled it into the bottom corner, before Johnson capped a fine display by poking home another Rydel delivery.

Five goals, another clean sheet and another great away day for the vocal Hatters supporters. We never stopped singing and Kath learnt a few new chants. Most of the second half saw us serenade the players with promotion songs. One fan got on the pitch before being told where to go by County fans losing patience with some recent bad behaviour by younger elements. Exiting the ground we noticed the ejected "fan" was still arguing with the cops. Alcohol was probably involved and it looked like he was on the threshold of a kicking by the Old Bill or detainment in Barnet overnight.

A quick getaway is never possible in London traffic but it didn't take long to ditch the car at the hotel and get the train to St Pancreas. One stop up to Angel on the tube and a meet up at a Mexican in Islington with Daniela. Top scran, Mexican beer and peppery tequila went down just nicely. Another win away, another reason to be cheerful.

CHAPTER SEVEN
February 2022

Tuesday 1st February 2022
Cheshire Senior Cup Quarter Final
Nantwich Town 1 County 2

Up for the cup again as County cross Cheshire to re-visit the venue of our Cheshire Senior Cup victory when we beat Tranmere in 2016 to lift the trophy. This might be a niche cup but nevertheless one worth winning. Tranmere still compete in this one along with Crewe as the only two league sides in the competition. Tranmere are currently second in League 2 while Alex languish at the bottom of League 1. If this competition is good enough for them it's good enough for us.

Nantwich currently reside in the relegation zone of the Northern Premier League. Their nickname is the Dabbers, a reference to the towns tanning industry or leather making history. If you have bought this book, you are probably someone who may be interested in these details. The Dabbers were formed in 1884 only a year after us. We were called Heaton Norris Rovers back then.

If I wasn't collating this log (of possibly one of our best ever campaigns) I might not have attended this evening. The plan of course is to attend as many matches as possible this season. I'm on holiday in Gran Canaria for a week later this month so will miss a couple of games. A bit of sun proving an irresistible draw. Plus it is half term at college/ Uni so my two sons are joining us in a diminishing opportunity for a family holiday. Both are now vacationing with groups of mates in the main.

One fellow who won't be here tonight is John Rooney. John has returned to Barrow for an undisclosed fee. Reports are that we have recouped most of our outlay. It is a high earner off the books and good for both parties. Under lockdown football John was a star for us. Since DC took over as manager the midfield triumvirate of Collar, Croasdale and Sarcevic have been so good that John can't get in the team.

The Weaver Stadium is a neat non-league affair. These games may prove to be cherished experiences. We look like we are on course for a return to the football league where we will leave these visits to non-league outposts behind. We've been pretty much everywhere on this journey to the centre of the earth. Or our unstoppable drop through the leagues. In the National North we had the misfortune to lose at Vauxhall Motors and at home to Rushall Olympic. Proper non-league. A crazy demise from our point of view. With no disrespect to any of the fine clubs we have played.

County have a new signing, the interestingly named Myles Hippolyte. Myles joins County from League Two Scunthorpe United on a free transfer. An experienced left sided forward who has also played number ten. I blustery night see's our team jog out in all blue with the home side in all green. I take a pew in the main stand. A decent structure similar to the one at Curzon Ashton. The opposite side has a small roof spanning two thirds of the length of the pitch which houses our drummer and singers. About 400 spectators have made the effort including an impressive 200 County fans.

Our line-up includes Ross, Keane, Minihan, Jennings, Newby and Reid. The rest plus the bench are academy players. Several have already shone this season including Alli, Edwards and Holding. County have the better of the opening exchanges but Nantwich take the lead after fifteen minutes through Argentinian Montefiori. The Dabbers fans have christened him the Cheshire Messi.

The temperature drops and I retreat downstairs into the bar for a relieving hot brew. I nearly had a Bovril. Then reminded myself that every time I have one I instantly regret it. If I want to melt my taste buds with the flavour of burning tar, I certainly don't want to pay for it when I could have a normal brew.

It looked like we wouldn't score. This would potentially be a ninth win in a row in all competitions. Matching a club record. I had pangs of self-doubt about whether it would have been worth the trip if we lose. The drive was longer than I thought. But a goal would warm the soul. I had to wait until the seventy-fourth minute when Reid turned in a cross that was glanced on by Jennings. We had more chances. The players and fans hoped we wouldn't go into extra time. Attendance of Cheshire Cup matches is pretty hardcore without the game being extended.

Fortunately, in the last-minute Newby floated a cross over for Reid to nod in from close range. You can't beat a last-minute winner, even in the Cheshire Cup. Next Tuesday see's us play Chesterfield in the biggest game of the season so far. Tonight is much less important. However, we have now progressed to the semi-final. It would be nice to win the treble of the League, FA Trophy and Cheshire Senior Cup. I mulled over the permutations on the way home. One for the connoisseur tonight, but worth the trip.

Saturday 5th February 2022
County 1   Dover Athletic 0

If there was ever a nailed-on win this is it. Unstoppable County versus desperate Dover. Dover aren't even desperate anymore they are doomed. Cut adrift at the bottom by thirty points. Including points deducted due to transgressions from last season. Close to or already mathematically relegated. Such is the relentlessness of our recent form compared to Dover's fate that defeat today would be a major shock. We need to be on our guard and remember the three points are key. 1-0 will do.

I wrote the above before kick-off. Recent form would suggest an easier victory. Fair play to Dover, they put in a mammoth defensive performance. They defended so deep at one point their back line was inside their eighteen-yard box. It was a siege with their defensive line in retreat on the precipice of the white cliffs of Dover. It was an ideal scenario for them. Nothing expected from the game, new recruits recently signed, an experienced manager in Andy Hessenthaler with difficult drizzly conditions.

The Pop Side was packed with plenty of school children which is always good to see. The youngsters and their parents boosted the crowd to an excellent 7,269 with 59 Dover loyalists. Chesterfield is a sell-out on Tuesday with 10,000 tickets sold. Great times to be a County fan. For fans that endured four seasons in the National League North, this is a transformation.

Sarcevic was out injured which made a difference in hindsight. Antoni has been the one with the guile in midfield to unlock a defence. The challenge was to get past a ten-man defence and another team of giants. The Whites were very physical and at times dirty. Hessenthaler had them fired up to upset the league leaders. The industrial tackling started early. Collar was hacked down needing treatment and was subbed in the second half. Hopefully not injured. Just before half time Dover's Judd hydroplaned across the saturated turf before taking Southam-Hales out with a two footed challenge. Straight red.

With the drizzle unrelenting there were a few impatient groans at half time. Fans can be impatient and used to winning. You have to dig a result out sometimes. The back of the Pop Side is geared up for the kids with a Junior zone and all manner of face painting etc. Good to see. Speaking with some parents there is a mix of County supporting fathers and mothers with City and United parenting too. I did take exception to the mother in a Liverpool bobble hat and scarf. Not a big deal but I'm sure the lady has other winter wear. We finally got to the head of the queue for food. They had run out of a few things through sheer demand. Good for the clubs coffers.

Second half we went straight on the attack. More penetration but hardly any clear-cut chances. Cross after cross went in as Dover's ten men camped themselves in their own half in stubborn resistance. Newby came on then Jennings. Nothing seemed to work as the clock ticked down. The drizzle persisted and the home fans were resigned to a disappointing draw. It was so tense I was squirming in my seat. Several times I held my head as a chance went wide.

Finally in the last five minutes Madden bundled the ball over the line from another corner. The ground exploded with relief and celebration. Chesterfield won again and we needed this victory to stay top of the league. Emotions were transformed in a way that only football can deliver. As we walked through the drizzle back to the car the feeling was one of joy rather than frustration. We need to get used to this now we are in a battle for top spot and automatic promotion.

Tuesday 8th February 2022
County 2   Chesterfield 2

We've had some mammoth cup matches this season against Bolton and Rotherham. Massive away followings and brilliant performances. The match tonight though is undoubtably the biggest match of the season so far. The table topping Hatters versus the second place Spireites. We are at the business end of the season. Still plenty of matches to go but we have got ourselves to the top and we plan to stay there. Chesterfield recently lost their manager but they have carried on winning. James Rowe was dismissed for serious indiscipline.

The Spireites have other concerns rumbling under the surface. In 2020 the club was bought by a community trust. Surprisingly, the cash strapped club managed to sign Kabongo Tshimanga from Boreham Wood for an undisclosed fee and a high wage package. A player that was being pursued by league clubs. A good bit of business with Kabongo prolific this season. Meanwhile they crowd funded frost covers even with FA Cup revenue from Chelsea away and last season furloughed players. Their social media is poorly updated and recently they somehow forgot to apply the frost covers pre match and only an army of volunteers and hot water saved the game.

Regardless of the Spireites amateurishness in certain departments, that man Tshimanga has been lethal and the team sit second in the league. With 1,500 away supporters in Edgeley Park the atmosphere will be electric. Walking towards the ground an extra buzz is in the air. The spotlights glisten casting light over the stands drawing the people to the spectacle. Turning the corner from the terraced streets Edgeley Park stands proud. The refurbished Cheadle End with the big new letters spelling Edgeley Park. The main stand with the classic old signage pronouncing Stockport County AFC.

The Pop Stand is packed. We sit in our official seats. Sometimes we sit near them. Tonight is a sell-out so we politely make sure we are not in someone else's seat. The attendance of 10,236 is our biggest home league crowd since Leeds in 2008. The Chesterfield fans to our right are in fine voice. Most of them are in the open Railway End. To our left the Cheadle End is bouncing. In our section the singers are equally determined to drown out the visitors.

The first half was a bit of a disaster. There was dubious officiating. The atmosphere was crackling. One of those nights where usually calm fans around us were jumping up and down and singing. A crunch match. We huffed and puffed with crosses going astray and too many high balls. The injured Sarcevic would have added more guile in midfield. Chesterfield were organised and fast on the break. Tshimanga the main threat. Jonnie must have wondered when I was going to stop waxing lyrical about him.

My worries materialised when a chipped ball into our box saw that man Tshimanga convert an over the shoulder volley. Quality I must admit. Five minutes later and only twenty minutes into the first half a deflected shot flat footed Hinchliffe in our goal for 0-2. The Spireites seemed to think the game was won and their policy became one of play acting and physicality. They started to spoil the game with tackles that went over the threshold and designed to wind us up.

Challinor must have given a reality check to our lads at half time. We needed to compose ourselves and play the game not the occasion. County did and the second half performance was much improved. Within four minutes we were assisted by their fullback King getting himself sent off for a two footed challenge on Rydel. Around us this was greeted with loud cheers. King was on our side in the first half and tried to wind us up by making 1-0 then 2-0 signs. This sign language meant King got dogs abuse from our section. I have no sympathy for him.

On the hour, Collar curled a long range shot past the keeper. Edgeley Park exploded. Five minutes later Croasdale smashed another long range shot into the bottom left-hand corner of the Chesterfield goal. The roof nearly came off the Pop Side. There was only going to be one winner now. Our opponents time wasted and their players went down injured resulting in ten minutes of injury time. County pressed and pressed and pumped in several corners. The last kick of the game was a zipped cross nearly headed in by Quigley. The ref blew for full time. The Spireites celebrated like they'd won the league.

Another amazing match in a season of amazing matches. The atmosphere was amazing too.

Saturday 12th February 2022
FA Trophy
County 1   Cheshunt 0

Another home game provides lower league opposition in the cup. We are having a favourable run in this competition. With the exception of Grimsby, today will be our third encounter against teams two or three levels below us in the pyramid. The gap is similar to a Premier League team playing a League 1 or League 2 side in the FA Cup. Cheshunt are two levels below us. They lie mid-table in the Isthmian Premier League. Isthmus is Greek for an area of land. In Cheshunt's case this pertains to the greater London and southeast counties.

I am enjoying these cup runs. For the benefit of this book it provides interesting content for me (and hopefully the reader). The priority is the league but writing this log has motivated me to attend all the cup matches in three competitions. Something I have never completed before.

This provides the chance to see and visit teams I have never seen before and will never see again. Teams who typically have been formed for as long as County. Cheshunt had a more recent birth in 1946. Their location is northeast of London just inside the Hertfordshire border. Geographically and traditionally a corridor for Spurs fans.

The Cheshunt Ultra's, a tongue in cheek moniker for their vocal supporters, are opposite me from my perch in the main stand. There are about 250 of them which is their average home attendance. This is probably the biggest game in their history. We are only three games from Wembley with the victors of today's game in the quarter-final draw. The Ambers have defeated two National South teams in this cup run. This is unlikely to be easy. However, Dave Challinor has said a strong line-up will be selected. I get the feeling Dave would love a Wembley visit.

Pre-match I watched a heart-warming interview with the Ambers manager Craig Edwards. A real character with beard and impressive curly moustache. Craig thought our atmosphere versus Chesterfield was amazing and something you don't see in the Premier League. At our level and in the lower echelons of non-league 100% of the regular fans are invested in the team and the match. True supporters. You could say that at most Premier League matches a significant percentage of the crowd are just there for the event. Especially at the bigger clubs. Of which many have no connection with the area that the clubs are in or the history or nuances of watching the team. This is illustrated by the fact most Premier League teams have doubled their average attendances since the birth of the Premier League. It has become a far more commercial and global entity. I prefer lower league.

Football after all is best appreciated through the nuances. The pain of never winning anything. The joy of eventually winning something. The frustration of play-off losses. The elation of beating relegation. The Premier League has become a groundhog day for most teams. Only the few will ever win it. Many are stuck in a midtable vacuum. The prize being entry into a dull competition such as the Europa League. Whereby too many boring matches are played for the sole reason of cash generation. If you sneak into the top four you dine at the top table of greed. The clubs would forgo winning the FA Cup for entry into what is the underachievers version of the true European Cup. A competition created for champions but often won by a team that finished third or fourth.

Rant over I take satisfaction from attending a down to earth football match today. County would love a trip to Wembley and it is great to see Cheshunt enjoying a trip to Edgeley Park with the chance of an upset. There is a drizzle like a persistent low-pressure shower drifting in at an angle. I hoped for a dry day for our southern visitors but typical northern conditions greeted them. The Cheshunt Ultra's are in fine voice though. They have their mascot with them. A lion dressed in the club colours of amber and chocolate who conducts the choir.

The County line-up has nine changes made up of fringe first teamers and two academy starlets. Edwards at full back and Cody Johnson in midfield. Johnson was worth the admission fee on his own. The sixteen-year-old debutant was man of the match. I magnificent achievement and a rare occasion when a home-grown talent makes an instant impact. I would go as far as to say Cody displayed the best debut I have ever seen at County from a youth player. Composed, moving the ball around with ease without mistakes. For his small stature he was strong in the tackle and won headers. Cody also directed the senior players around him showing them where he was moving the ball linking defence to attack. Sam Minihan was captain for the day in recognition of his 200th appearance.

County were below par in the first half. Ollie Crankshaw was unusually wasteful and inaccurate with shots. Alex

Reid made little impact and Kitching struggled to deliver any telling balls into the danger area. After a reset at half time we improved in the second half. Cheshunt were solid but showed little goal threat so the game was there for the taking. The drizzle stopped but the temperature was still Baltic. The Cheshunt Ultra's were undeterred banging out a constant rhythm.

Whitfield came on as sub. On the hour mark Ben flicked the ball on for Hippolyte to score from twelve yards. Reid was subbed for the promising Millenic Alli who made more of an impact. After eighty-three minutes Ross was sent off. Our goalie rushed out to the edge of his box and the ball appeared to unluckily bounce off his chest onto his arm. Hinchliffe went into the nets as we subbed Crankshaw. Down to ten men County saw the game out.

Highlight of the day was undoubtably the impressive debut by Cody Johnson. Followed by the Cheshunt Ultra's. Ben Whitfield has come back after injury and County are in the quarter-finals. Not a classic but plenty of positives.

Tuesday 15th February 2022
Bromley 1   County 3

Where is Bromley? I know as I've been there for work but for most it could be anywhere around the southeast sprawl near London. It is further than predicted. Think London and the quick calculation is a 200-mile journey then it gets tricky depending which side of the capital. North London is relatively straight forward. Bromley isn't. My destination is buried in the southeast London suburbs towards Croydon. 240 miles and it is those extra 40 miles that are the issue. They are slow ones as you navigate the M25 and the Dartford crossing. All for a good cause. Super Stockport County.

This one is another hard-core excursion for the County faithful. A long one even for a Saturday. This is a Tuesday so even more commitment. I'm only doing one leg of the journey today. I'm stopping over with a work call en-route. The fact we are doing so well will attract extra County fans. There are a number of exiles who attend the southern matches too. But the distance combined with a Tuesday night means anything over 350 County fans would be impressive.

Most footy fans are into stadiums. Some are obsessed. I fall somewhere in between. I'll take a diversion to check out a new ground on my travels. Usually I'll drive around it or walk if necessary to check out the stands. Some are more determined to get inside and some are part of the 92 club. The members have visited all 92 league grounds. Something that was a fixed challenge before non-league teams were allowed promotion into the Football League. That started somewhere in the late 80's. Since then the 92 has become a moving challenge as two clubs move up and down.

Tonight is a new ground for me and a fixture I was determined to attend. Hayes Lane (or the renamed Courage Stadium) looks characterful. These days we have the benefit of google maps, the internet and last season the live streams. So you can get a good look at a ground virtually. In the old days (or pre mobile phones and the internet) life involved greater anticipation. You had to physically go somewhere to check it out. Photographic football books were few and far between.

My destination is well worth the visit. As described by Mike Bayly in his brilliant book British Football's Greatest Grounds- "Hayes Lane is different. On the narrow track leading off the main road to the ground is a paddock with grazing horses. For a location in London fare zone five this is most unanticipated." The surroundings are pleasantly leafy. Most London grounds are hemmed in by shops and houses, train tracks, excessive traffic, impossible parking and in many cases run down streets. All that glitters is not gold. London is a magnificent city but greater London is not necessarily beautiful. Hayes Lane is a pleasant exception. If you buy Mike's book you will find a hundred picturesque and characterful football grounds from around the British Isles.

A nice feature of tonight's visit is the standing terrace that runs the full length of the pitch. A rarity. Great examples from the past are the Kippax and the Longside at Man City and Burnley. Now consigned to the history books and replaced with much less characterful structures. At Hayes Lane, the terrace is uncovered. Not on the scale of the aforementioned examples but a thing of beauty.

Predictably the journey is littered with delays. Sixty mile an hour variable speed limits and the Dartford crossing in drizzly conditions. On arrival, there is indeed a paddock and leafy environs as mentioned by Mike Bayly. The ground has been redeveloped with a new seated stand behind one of the goals incorporating a sports centre. Plus a neat main stand. Then the full-length open terrace and partially covered home terrace behind the other goal. There is a big crowd of 2,700 for the Lillywhite's. Including an impressive 430 County fans. A mixture of long-distance travellers and exiles. To our right an excitable bunch of teenage home fans who regale us with various chants about us being northern and paying our benefits. We respond with laughter and waves.

County, resplendent in pink away shirts, dominated the opening exchanges. Bromley have the best home record in the league but looked like the away side by defending deep. County continued to carve out chances and control midfield with an excellent display but couldn't break the deadlock. The drizzle persisted at an angle directly towards the County fans. Such was the impressive nature of our play this wasn't a problem. At half time, the away following were in good spirits albeit a bit damp.

The second half followed in the same vein with more impressive pressing and wide play creating chances. Bromley started to resist but the deadlock was broken when Madden headed home a pinpoint cross from Southam-Hales. This silenced the Bromley fans as we serenaded them with our "we always win away" song. The Lillywhite's stirred into attacking intent perhaps realizing that the formidable opposition are top of the table for a reason. In the first half our hosts looked as if they would be happy with a 0-0. This was countered with another goal by the mighty Hatters. A contender for goal of the season. The hard-working Quigley decided to go direct and blast an unstoppable twenty-five yarder into the net.

With five minutes to go Madden got his brace by hooking one home from inside the box to make it three. Bromley captain Webster took his frustration out by smashing an unstoppable twenty yarder in for a consolation in the last minute. Another superb performance by County against a promotion contender. Well worth the 480-mile round trip for the travellers from Stockport. I will do the second leg tomorrow as I'm staying in Dartford overnight with work.

A thoroughly enjoyable visit to Hayes Lane- a highly recommended ground to visit. Great result and more impressive football by County. The drizzle finally abated but the spirits were already lifted. Top of the league and we go again at home on Saturday versus Woking.

Saturday 19th February 2022
County 1   Woking 0

This week we had another favourable FA Trophy draw against the lowest ranked team left in the competition. Market Needham is another long jaunt, this time a 230 mile four hours plus journey. It's near Ipswich. I would have liked a visit but I have tickets for a gig so won't get back in time. I'm into lots of new bands but the entertainment will be a classic old band. The prog/rock slightly psychedelic Curved Air featuring the delectable Sonja Kristina. Songstress and ex-wife of Police drummer Stewart Copeland.

Enough of the musical musing, this is a footy book and today we are in league action against our visitors from sunny Surrey. Also known as the Cardinals or Cards. A cardinal is a bird but I don't believe they frequent the British Isles. Woking's nickname refers to the cardinal red colour of said birds. It feels American. There is the St Louis Cardinals baseball team. The colour is popular at American universities and connected to sorority Alpha Omicron Pi, a women's movement formed in the late 1800's. We now have an omicron variant virus. I digress. Let's just presume Woking's colours are cardinal red just because they like the colour.

Another healthy crowd of 6,800 filled a damp Edgeley Park. Persistent drizzle has prevailed over the last few days with high winds. Unusually the south of England has been hit harder than the north by a double header of storm Dudley, then storm Eunice. Not sure how they produce the names. There is probably a bowl full of storm balls at the met office where they have an FA Cup style draw. The first half was a damp squib. Woking were solid and we were wasteful. The ball spent a lot of time in the air. The only consolation being the appearance of blue skies over Edgeley. Like a meteorological miracle the sun shone brightly. The sun, a phenomenon I don't think we have seen for months. The clouds returned during half time but I consoled myself with the knowledge that this time next week, I'll be in Gran Canaria.

In contrast the second half was a humdinger. The sun reappeared and spirits were lifted. County looked a lot better and we soon carved out our first real chance of the day when Madden headed just over. Within ten minutes a melee ensued in front of the benches at the far side. Collar clearly pushed a Cards player resulting in a yellow. Then a bizarre five minutes was endured as the ref, linesman and fourth official had an extended conflab resulting in a straight red for Hogan. Liam was dismissed for foul and abusive language. This unexpectedly helped us. Crankshaw and Newby came on to provide speed on the counter-attack. Followed by more fresh and fast legs in the form of Kitching.

What followed was a brilliant ten man display for the remaining forty minutes. Woking gained confidence and went expansive allowing more space for County to exploit on the break. The Cards were energised. Their bench and players looked confident they could win it. But we stood firm and constantly fed Crankshaw and Newby to run at their defence. With eighteen minutes of normal time left, a trademark Palmer header was thumped into the net from a Rydel corner.

Woking were sapped of their energy. We started to dominate possession and had more chances with Crankshaw slipping twice when in a great position. Ollie and Newby continued to torment the Cards defence. Both were great at working the ball into the corners to run the clock down. With seven minutes added on, a nervous finale ensued but we held out.

A heroic second half performance. Chesterfield and Boreham Wood both lost to cap an excellent day. We now have a six-point gap at the top. The Wood still have four games in hand. If they win all four we still play them at home with a much better goal difference. It could be in our hands now if we continue our impressive trajectory under Dave Challinor.

Saturday 26th February 2022
County 1   Weymouth 0

So far, I've missed a few long distance away matches but I'm on a 90% plus attendance record. I'm going to cup matches including the FA Cup, FA Trophy and even the Cheshire Senior Cup. I'll rattle off somewhere in the region of sixty County games this season. I'm absent today as I have flown out to Gran Canaria for a week with the family. A half term break with my college and Uni attending sons and lovely wife. Not such a hardship.

The Strawberry Radio app has come to the rescue as I sit outside a bar looking at the beach. A benefit of these resorts is the cheap beer. My beer is 2 euro's a pint. I've been to some bars where it is more expensive to take a pee. That was Tenerife where the beer was a euro in happy hour and the tariff for the loo was 1.50. I strange sort of recycling cost.

I like to strike up footy chat on holiday and spread the County word. Frustratingly, I had to provide a potted history of our trials and tribulations to a City fan who appeared oblivious to the last twenty years. I couldn't decide whether he was taking the mickey or being friendly. The fella seemed genuine and a match going Citizen. He remembered us beating them but had no idea how far we had fallen. I suppose we don't get coverage in the Manchester Evening News these days and most sky blues have revelled in Premier League glory for the last ten years. I was relieved when my new mate moved on.

Jon Keighren provided comfort with his familiar County tones on the Strawberry radio commentary. A little technical miracle with a strawberry icon staring at me from a small screen in my palm. In the middle of the Atlantic somewhere off the coast of Africa I am receiving frequencies from home. On the flight over I contemplated how a phone only 5mm thick could store all that information. Hours of downloaded music and apps and social media gubbins. I recalled the movie Tesla about Nikola Tesla who discovered the miracle of alternating current, a mysterious phenomenon. It is a little miracle for me to hear County coverage in the sun. After all, I'm old enough to remember when some people didn't even have land line phones.

Two beers in and a family passes by with the kids wearing City shirts. The holidaymakers are mainly Scandinavians. I wondered if the Ardwick FC / Man City loyalists were from within the boundaries of Mancunia. Or more likely Stopfordians. They sat near me. The excitable tones were to the tune of Ireland. Thick Irish, sounding like Cork or similar. As the match progressed our beloved Hatters seemed to be struggling and the excitement levels were low. My mind drifted to the nice Irish family. My Grandad once said- "if United don't shape themselves and City win a Premier League we'll have to keep an eye on them. We don't want them taking over and getting fans all over the place like us."

He never saw City win a Prem. I wonder what he would have thought of City's current Mancunian domination. Of course, I could remind anyone that County's latest record v the Citizens is won 3, drawn 2, lost 1. Which I have done on many occasions. Back to the match and it sounds like one we are going to have to dig out. There were a lot of long balls. The conditions were spring like, which means the temperature was probably around 14 degrees. It is 24 here which provided a surreal feel to tuning into a County match from the beach. Nothing seemed to happen until the Terra's Murray deflected into his own net.

The second half was a grinder. As in keeping it safe and protecting the three points. Another 1-0 home win against lowly opposition. You need these kind of results to win a league. I don't think I missed much. As the sun relentlessly radiated I decided to join the family on the beach. My lads decided that they would sooner generate a tan than sit in the shade tuning into the County frequencies. I was duly instructed to apply more suntan to my wife's back, then go to the shop for some beers for my lads.

Challinor was disappointed with the second half and especially the fact Kitching got himself sent off right at the end for squaring up to someone for a second yellow. We have won fifteen of the last sixteen matches. The best record in the top five divisions of English football. Incredible.

CHAPTER EIGHT
March 2022

Saturday 5th March 2022
Aldershot 0   County 2

I was really looking forward to today's visit to the Recreation Ground, a stadium I've never been to. I have ticked off in the region of seventy grounds over the years but this is one that got away. Probably because County have rarely played the Shots in recent history. I missed the away match a few years ago and the previous one was 2011. Before that you have to go back to 90/91 for our last visit. That trend will continue as I am on a return flight from the family break in Gran Canaria. Luckily, the match was selected for the telly on BT Sport so I can record it and watch tonight. I'll try to tune into the Strawberry Radio app en-route.

If you recall Southend away at the start of the season, I waxed lyrical about the barrel roofed stand that housed the County fans. The Recreation Ground has a barrel roof stand behind one of the goals. To its right there is a pitched roof stand. The roof is resplendent in red and blue stripes. The paint has faded adding to the genuine and characterful feel. If we get promoted I will still make a trip to see a match one day. If I win the lottery/ or when I retire, I am going to buy a camper van and tour the British Isles visiting the most characterful and picturesque grounds. Mixed in with some music festivals.

The week in Gran Canaria has been brilliant. Hotter than usual for February and not as windy. Apparently it gets really windy but we had unusually calm conditions. So much so we went sea fishing in what our hosts described as flat conditions. I would describe it as choppy to very choppy. So much so I barfed over the side. I caught a massive fish. I thought it was a big tuna but was informed it was a wounded amberjack. Meanwhile County played a mid-week behind closed doors friendly losing 2-1 to Salford. I good opportunity to look at our impressive youngsters and get the likes of Whitfield back to match fitness.

I was mid-air as County kicked off at 5:20pm live on BT Sports in Hampshire. As soon as we landed I switched off flight mode and checked the scores. 2-0 to County and Chesterfield only drew. We are now five points ahead of the Spireites with a game in hand. I got home and watched the match. Pre-recorded before we departed to the Canaries. In drizzly conditions an impressive 360 County fans can be heard loud and clear. In a similar vein to the Dagenham away match, the Hatters executed a perfect away performance.

Within twenty-five minutes we were 2-0 up. Crankshaw dinked one in, then Collar headed in after a cracking move before knee sliding towards the travelling fans in the corner. Our midfield dynamo could easily have made it three with another header just before the break. It was great to see Sarcevic back in the side after injury. With the Shots offering little goal threat, the second half was played out on cruise control.

Unfortunately, I missed out on an opportunity to visit the Recreation Ground. The consolation was a cracking family holiday and a dose of much needed winter sun. Life is good and County are on the up. The next morning, the sun is shining in Stockport. I'm at Edgeley Park for the programme and memorabilia faire. I'm selling off some programmes etc and my last book. All for a good cause. Proceeds go towards the proposed Danny Bergara statue.

Saturday 12th March 2022
FA Trophy Quarter Final
Needham Market 0 v County 3

My mid-season break continues. After missing the last two games as I was in Gran Canaria, this is one for radio again as I have tickets for a gig tonight. When I bought the tickets we were due to play Notts County at home so no problem. With today's fixture being near Ipswich, there is no chance of getting back to sunny Darwen tonight for the gig. We are seeing the legendary Curved Air at the Darwen Library Theatre, the nearest gig on the tour. So it is a date in deepest Lancashire.

I've made a rule in recent years that I won't see a band with members over sixty years old. That effectively rules out most bands active in the 80's. Scary thought really. The reasoning for this policy is that I would rather support new or young bands in pubs and clubs. I've seen most of the rock bands from the 80's anyway. Back when they were young and hungry. Even bands from the 90's are getting on a bit in rock and roll terms. Tonight is an exception. Occasionally there is a band that has a bit of cult status. Curved Air fall into that category. Fronted by singer Sonja Kristina, the band are purveyors of psychedelic/ prog/ rock / pop. A combo of sounds worth checking out live.

But first up is a cup quarter-final. The treble of league, FA Trophy and Cheshire Senior Cup is still on. The Cheshire Cup would be a nice bonus but not essential. The FA Trophy would form a genuine league and cup double. This competition has real pedigree with the final at Wembley which has attracted up to 53,000 fans in the past. With Notts County and Wrexham in the draw, there is potential for a bumper crowd at the final.

Down in sleepy Suffolk another great turnout of Hatters fans bolstered the crowd by 460 to 1,500. Supplemented by extra Marketmen fans for the occasion increasing their average 250 attendance six-fold. Being a rural non-league team I suspect their nickname has escaped any politically correct re-alignment. In a city the nickname would likely be adjusted to Marketpeople. The pitch looks half decent in the photographic coverage, allaying fears of turned ankles for our men in the league run-in. A strong line-up of first team squad members is supplemented by our impressive youngsters including Edwards, Cody Johnson and a debut for keeper Ashby-Hammond.

Away cup ties at small grounds can sometimes provide a slip up but County executed their game plan without hitches. On a bright day in front of their second highest ever crowd, Needham were outclassed. On twenty-five minutes Reid stooped to nod home from close range. Three minutes later, Keane unleashed a thirty-yard thunder-blaster past their keeper. On half-time Reid converted his brace latching onto a through ball by Josh Edwards. 3-0 at half-time and game over.

Into the semi-finals, no injuries and another clean sheet. That is four out of four clean sheets in this competition and we are now one match away from Wembley. I've lost track of how many wins we've had. Only the draw at home to Chesterfield interrupted our relentless winning streak. Amazing times.

The Fingerpost Flyer supporters coach had to be pulled out of soft ground. Being in Suffolk, a tractor was on hand to rescue the loyal supporters. The Marketmen's neighbours Ipswich Town nicknamed the Tractor Boys, possibly on hand as the local rescue service. Later in deepest Lancashire, Kath and I enjoyed a delectable display of psychedelic tuneage. Another County victory and a great gig. The perfect type of day.

Tuesday 15th March 2022
County 3   Notts County 0

I'm back after a bit of a break. Suntan fading but reinvigorated after some winter sun. Not that I needed much reinvigoration. The luxury of a Canaries visit was welcome. However, the season has been so good since Dave Challinor took over that the sun has been metaphorically shining on County ever since. Even though we have only recently started to see the sun again in our north-westerly skies as we pull away from winter. The future is bright and the future is this County side relentlessly progressing in the league and cups.

Tonight provides a real challenge with the visit of the Magpies. A big team with a big away following pushing for the play-offs. Consensus is that they will come for a draw. They need points to get into the play-off places and a point would represent a good one tonight against the table-toppers. We are not going to win every match. Our run is unprecedented but there will surely be some dropped points. There is a buzz around Stockport and a big crowd is expected. Another fan march has been organised from the Armoury pub all along Castle Street to the ground. The fans are the twelfth man.

I checked and we have won sixteen out of the last seventeen games drawing the other. Amazing. Another fixture has been added after we were drawn away to Wrexham in the semi-final of the F A Trophy. Another humdinger of a game for the diary. Tonight there's another bumper crowd of just short of 8,000. Surprisingly, there are only 450 Notts fans, possibly due to a bit of disillusionment with their struggle to get into the play-off spots. I checked out the fan march as it progressed towards the ground. At the front, the fans held a fifty-foot-wide County scarf. The drummer pounded away in a continental style rhythm. There was pyro, blue smoke and loud chants. Impressive.

Today, the council confirmed the 250-year lease of Edgeley Park to the football club protecting our future. We seem a million miles away from our tribulations. Not only on the pitch but from the historical shadow of Sale Rugby Club and their takeover of our holy ground. Now we truly own the stadium and control our destiny. With the finance of our saviour Mr Stott, we are on a trajectory that we could only dream of a few years ago.

In the Pop Side many held aloft the programme in support of the people of Ukraine. The centre pages have temporarily become a Ukrainian flag. On the pitch the players continued their relentless march. Notts had a couple of early chances but other than that, it was one-way traffic. After half an hour the mercurial Madden nodded home a Southam Hales cross. On fifty minutes Hinchliffe's pinpoint clearance found Paddy Madden who flicked on for Crankshaw to fire home. Madden scored again after seventy minutes, slotting home from twelve yards after a Hippolyte cross. Paddy was man of the match and must be favourite for Player of the Year.

Another fantastic victory. Dave Challinor must be on his way to having a stand named after himself. Paddy Madden is on his way to becoming an all-time County legend. That's seventeen wins and a draw out of the last eighteen matches. County are making football history.

Saturday 19th March 2022
County 4   Wealdstone 2

I'm with a mate today who hasn't been for a while. Certainly not since the Challinor revolution. He will be in for a treat watching the new County. I've done some distance watching County this season. My app says its past 4,500 miles but it must be more than that. This doesn't include the additional diversions or what some would consider mad cross-country journeys. For example, the Woking away game when I travelled straight over to Yeovil after the match for a works exhibition. Then back home the next evening. Or staying in Dartford for work and going over to the Bromley away game. Back home the next day. Then the following day up to Newcastle upon Tyne with work.

It's all worth it though once the boys in blue (or pink) run on the pitch. As one lad said at Bromley away, "it's a five hour journey each way, I'll get back about 2am, I'm in work at 7am but I love it." Following a football team on long away journeys is something fans from all corners of the country do every week. I suppose it is something that's in your blood. Most people would consider it mad. But for me, it is an experience. Not just the football. It's visiting different places and meeting fans and the banter. I'm going the extra yard for this book. Some do it every season.

Today we play the Stones. At the away match you may recall I was nursing a hangover in Baltic conditions and purchasing the worst burger I've ever had. Or ever had one bite of. The football was better as we won 4-1 including an Ollie Crankshaw hattrick. The dominance of our performance against Notts on Tuesday resulted in total submission by the Magpies. The quality of our opposition today is inferior so in theory we should be in for another good day. Whichever way you cut it; it's difficult not to sound cocky at the moment. Let's say confident. After what we've been through in the last ten years, I might as well enjoy the moment.

Another good crowd greets us today. Just under 7,500 and about 200 from northwest London. The travelling Stones fans are making a bit of a racket and quite impressive. One of the good things about being in the Pop Side is the banter with the adjacent away fans. Our visitors got plenty of opportunity to give us some stick in the first half too. The form book went out the window. After a bright start we conceded two goals. On the unlucky thirteenth minute

Stones defender Cook headed home from a free kick. The Stones were on a roll and fired another couple of chances over the bar at the Railway End. Just after half an hour Wealdstone got a second from a curling free kick that tucked into the top left-hand corner of our net.

The crowd was in shock as the script was torn up. The Stones fans serenaded us with "top of the league you're having a laugh." Half time was a relief to hopefully provide a re-group. In true Challinor style, the managers work was done within the fifteen-minute break and the script was re-written. The first half was not a reflection of the final manuscript. In the second period, County blew away the Stones with the performance of champions elect. In an amazing sequence we scored three goals in seven minutes to take the lead. Madden converted a pen after a hand ball on fifty-five minutes. Two minutes later, Madden turned provider – sending over a low delivery from the left that was converted by Johnson.

Palmer scored another header from a Sarcevic corner to complete the turnaround. An incredible seven minutes of football. Sarc cheekily cupped his ears to the Stones contingent during the goal celebration. Several irate away fans charged to the front gesticulating towards our midfield maestro. Some "souvenirs" were thrown by the frustrated Stones fans. We serenaded the visiting contingent with an ironic version of "top of the league we're having a laugh." Great when you can chuck the opposition fans chants back at them.

County weren't finished. Sarcevic fired home an angled effort from the left to make it four after Collar had struck the upright. What a comeback and what a match. County proved again that they have an indomitable spirit. This one could have been a blip letting the chasing pack back in. But County stuck at it and blew the Stones away maintaining the seven-point gap at the top of the table.

On a beautiful spring day a thoroughly enjoyable match was enjoyed by another bumper crowd at Edgeley Park. Great fight back and a great atmosphere. My mate was well impressed.

Tuesday 22nd March 2022
Kings Lynn Town 0 County 3

Nice long drive on a weeknight to the deepest depths of Norfolk. It is a market town and a port. Or should I say the River Great Ouse has slashed a path through the northern coast of Norfolk and stopped at my destination. So about as much of a port as Salford Quays. It's about ten miles in land. I suppose you could call it an inland port. During the First World War, King's Lynn was one of the UK's first towns to suffer aerial bombing by a naval Zeppelin, commanded by Captain Lieutenant Magnus von Platen-Hallermund. Eleven bombs were dropped. Not much has happened there since. Perhaps the most significant event being tonight's visit of the mighty Stockport County.

Kings Lynn are second bottom twelve points from safety and probably already preparing for next season in the National North. There is no such thing as a guaranteed three points but the form book suggests otherwise. We've won nineteen of our last twenty matches in all competitions and fourteen out of fifteen in the league. The Linnets have only won two in ten, although they got a good 3-0 win away to Aldershot on Saturday. These lot should be put to the sword.

The trip itself falls into the most hard-core matches of the season category for those attending. The schlep across Woodhead, around Sheffield across Lincolnshire and to the top of Norfolk is not easy. Especially on a Tuesday requiring most to take time off work. There won't be many exiles present presuming the greatest location for migration must be the southeast and London. We do have exiles around the country but north Norfolk is unlikely to be a major catchment area. I'm doing another combo with work and stopping near sunny Lynn. You've got be mad as a hatter. Which I probably am.

The journey across the flatlands of Lincolnshire was a bit surreal. I've been around the east of England before but I forgot how flat it is. It just keeps going to the horizon, flat as a pancake. Nearing the border with Norfolk there's a small hamlet of truck stops and diners with an American style motel. Just like the Bates Motel in the Psycho movie. I am in England but not typical England. It feels a bit Route 66. Just inside Norfolk lies Kings Lynn. My hotel is across an iron bridge straddling the River Great Ouse. It's the kind of place where big boats drop things off and collect stuff from factories and warehouses. I suppose it does what inland ports do.

Yesterday I circumnavigated the online ticket site. An experience akin to a game of Pac-Man. Similar to the Alty away match I chased blue dots around the seating plan and eventually managed to bag two seats for Wrexham away in the F A Trophy semi-final. Somehow another 1,249 fans managed to decipher the system to make it a sell-out to season ticket holders. We are one step from Wembley but with the formidable hurdle of the Red Dragons away. A magical double (or even triple if you include the Cheshire Cup) is a possibility. But I'd settle for promotion alone. And that is tonight's objective- another three points to keep that gap going at the top.

The ground is in a nice residential area in contrast to the industrial setting for my hotel. I circumnavigated the stadium. I do this for any new ground. I have wanted to visit since I watched the behind closed doors lockdown match last season. The place feels like an old league ground. It has an impressively large and grand main stand. Down one side is a covered terrace, an open terrace behind one goal and just a wall behind the other with a tiny terrace. You can look over the wall for a free view. On one side of the ground is a park with wide pathways. Probably providing the idea to call the stadium The Walks.

There are 274 County fans here according to official sources but it looks like more. We have part of one side, some behind the goal and fans in the seats in the main stand. There are only 914 in total with the home fans probably resigned to relegation. I'm peckish but can tell through experience that the food kiosk is a slow server. The queue provides a good view but similar to Colne away last season it will probably take most of the first half to get served. On the pitch the County machine is in its typically efficient state. Resplendent in pink we dash around the pitch leaving the Linnets as blue shadows. Challinor has made several changes designed to rest players such as Sarcevic.

Minihan, Hogan, Quigley and Newby all get a start. Southam-Hales is not in the squad and the bad news comes through post-match that Macauley has an ACL injury and may not return this season. Faith was repaid as both Hogan and Newby bagged first half goals. Newby tapped in a Kitching shot that was going wide. Then Newby assisted Hogan from a corner which Hoges nodded in. Lynn were plucky but the Hatters were too good.

Second half our domination continued. Only six minutes in Quigley drove towards the goal breaking free before being cropped from behind. Straight red. The talisman Madden dispatched the free kick perfectly into the bottom corner of the net. Match over County didn't relent and kept pressing. The Linnets showed spirit but couldn't keep up with their superior visitors. Another great away performance opening up a ten-point gap at the top of the league.

Saturday 26th March 2022
Eastleigh 0   County 2

One of the benefits of our non-league journey to the centre of the earth is you get to visit multiple new places most seasons. If you keep getting yourselves relegated on a regular basis then finally get promoted the rollercoaster of fixtures keeps changing. How boring it must be to watch Everton or Arsenal. Never relegated and been in the same division for hundreds of years playing the same teams ad infinitum. Ok, they have promoted teams coming up but in recent history that's just been a revolving door of Fulham, Norwich and West Brom. County on the other hand have had a new selection of opponent nearly every year for ten years.

The lower you fall the smaller the teams are. At our nadir we even started to play village teams and works teams (Vauxhall Motors for God's sake). Which leads me to today's opponents the Spitfires of Eastleigh. Where is Eastleigh? At least in the Football League you know what to expect. Most people are familiar with the destinations. Rochdale-up north, sounds Victorian, probably not beautiful. Portsmouth- south coast, nice harbours, bit rough round the edges. Cambridge-university town, got to be nicer than Rochdale. Barnsley-Rochdale with a different accent. Hartlepool- somewhere near Geordieland, they hang monkeys.

Down here in non-league it's all an adventure. Eastleigh is near Southampton. As previously mentioned, they are called the Spitfires. Something to do with the first one being flown from the local aerodrome. Another south coast visit testing the tachometer. This season has been a real challenge for the away fan. Just check out this list of long-distance adventures (in miles from sunny Stocky)-

Dover 311, Torquay 260, Weymouth 260, Eastleigh 245, Southend 240, Bromley 240, Yeovil 230, Aldershot 220,

Woking 220. Not to mention the other London teams and Kings Lynn! Don't forget to add on the return leg.

The Spitfires are down in eighteenth but pretty much safe fifteen points clear of Weymouth who would need promotion form to catch our hosts. You could surmise various permutations to our opponents approach. Factors include- players playing for new contracts, wanting the scalp of the mighty County and playing without pressure. Which means they are unlikely to be pushovers. Their manager is journeyman ex-footballer and former City player Lee Bradbury. Apparently he was in the army before his football career so should have them well drilled.

Intentions were to attend today but another musical intervention occurred. Just as well really as I was away in Birmingham at the NEC with work Thursday/ Friday and Kings Lynn on Tuesday at the match. There are only so many miles one can accrue without it becoming daft. Tonight I have tickets for The Chats at the Academy. I youthful trio of Aussie nutters who have risen from antipodean pubs and BBQ parties to headlining the big Academy in rapid time. Mainly due to their humorous pop punk/ rock tunes. So some beers and pogoing later.

Jon Keighren will provide the analysis and commentary. Down on the sunny south coast at the Silverlake Stadium not much seems to be happening in the first half. It sounds like an untypically flat performance by the Hatters. The only analysis being that we are pumping long balls up to Madden and Quigley and giving the ball away. Co-commentator and County reporter Sam Byrne is describing the performance as the flattest since Dave Challinor took over. Fortunately, DC is a master at half time team talks and substitutions so I'm not too worried. But it would be great to get three points and celebrate with a few pre-gig beers in Manchester.

Four minutes into the second half Hippolyte smashed a strike from just outside the box to score. Followed by a cartwheel celebration in front of the travelling fans. Just what the doctor ordered. Amazingly Wrexham are losing 2-4 at home to Dover and Halifax are 0-1 down! Sarcevic hits the bar after juggling with the ball. Challinor has worked his magic at half time. Then Hogan headed home from a Sarcevic corner with seven minutes to go before racing around the advertising hoardings celebrating with the County fans. That secured a 2-0 victory. Halifax lost, Chesterfield and Notts drew their match while Wrexham somehow won 6-5.

That's now a club record nine away wins in a row and ten wins in a row in all competitions. Twenty wins overall in the last twenty-one matches. Phenomenal form. Ben Hinchliffe notched up his one hundredth clean sheet for County. Top of the league and unchartered territory for us. Never mind having such a gap at the top, we've rarely ever been top of a league in living memory (or the last fifty years). The record itself must be reaching a level of most wins in a given period in the history of football by any team!

Tuesday 29th March 2022
Cheshire Senior Cup Semi Final
County 5 Crewe Alexandra 0

We play our old Cheshire rivals Crewe tonight as we go for the treble. We haven't played Alex in a truly meaningful match for what must be about twelve years. They've survived in the league while we embarked on our vertical journey down the pyramid. Some statistically savvy supporters may be able to uncover some fixture we have had (probably in this cup) but I'm not going to check. I'm pretty hard-core but I have my boundaries. Crewe languish bottom of League 1 almost mathematically relegated. Nevertheless they ply their trade two leagues above us. Our team is full of League 1 pedigree so I expect a close match tonight.

I'm in my cup match perch in the Main Stand. An alternative view from the Pop Side. Variation is the spice of life. My ticket is right next to the tunnel. A good view of the players close up. Now we are a team to be proud of I must admit to getting a childlike tingle of excitement at seeing the County heroes. The likes of Madden have put in such a shift that grown men shout come on Paddy as he emerges from the retractable tunnel. And kids cheer and shout and scramble for autographs. It really is a brilliant time to be a County fan. Tonight the Main Stand and the lower tier of the Cheadle End are open providing potential for around 5,500 supporters. It is the Cheshire Cup so we are unlikely to get near that figure.

A small number of Alex fans have made the trip. They've had a dispiriting season so only the hardy will have bothered. I'd say there are about 80 across in the Pop Side to supplement the 1,200 hardcore County fans. The loyalists were rewarded with another impressive performance. The Railwaymen included several youngster while we made eleven changes. Such is the depth of our squad we still fielded a team that easily beat our visitors. The starting line-up included our deadline day signings. Courtney Duffus (striker on loan from Morecambe), Andy Cannon (midfielder signed from Hull) and Zaine Francis-Angol (defender on loan from Hartlepool). Plus Crankshaw, Newby, Reid, Keane, Jennings and the superb young talent Cody Johnson.

Crewe looked quick and pressed well in the early stages. They are a League 1 side and will be recruiting good level prospects. Our youngsters Pye and Johnson were a match supplemented by the senior squad players and new signings. County soon got on top and created chances. New boy Cannon fired home from twelve yards to open the scoring. Newby in particular looked lively while Cody Johnson glided across the pitch. What a prospect he is. Crankshaw crossed before a defender knocked in an own goal. 2-0 at half time.

Second half Jennings converted an early pen before heading home a Newby corner for his brace. Duffus up front looked lively but was slightly off the pace as he recovers from illness. New fullback Francis-Angol looked quality. The other new recruit Andy Cannon was the standout. Full of running and tackling. The scoring was complete when Reid had a shot deflected in for 5-0. The crowd was well entertained and the Cheadle End was bouncing. The feel-good factor is in full flow at County. The winning streak continues and the treble is on.

Vauxhall Motors are our opponents in the final. Saturday is another semi-final away at Wrexham. That will be a stiffer test but with this County side all comers seem to be defeated. Is it possible to just keep winning? The run of victories is getting to unprecedented levels and this journey just keeps getting better.

CHAPTER NINE
April 2022

Saturday 2nd April 2022
FA Trophy Semi-Final
Wrexham 2   County 0

This is one of those matches that gives you a real buzz. Away match at a big rival in a semi-final. 12:30 kick off on police advice with Jonnie at a match that will have an electric atmosphere. 1,260 County fans in a sold-out allocation (we could have sold 3,000) against a promotion challenger with a chance of an appearance at Wembley. It doesn't get much better than this. The local constabulary decided on denying the chance for away supporters to imbibe excessive amounts of pre-match alcohol. This could have resulted in a cocktail of trouble as the table topping Cheshire visitors made the short journey across the Cymru border.

The Red Dragons have famously been bought by Deadpool star Ryan Reynolds and Hollywood royalty partner Rob McElhenney. An odd couple with no previous soccer knowledge attracted by the working-class town appeal of Wrexham and a probably dubious family tree link to Wales. With awkward brand promotion the film stars have bizarrely been involved in anything from TikTok to Ifor Williams livestock trailers. Meanwhile Hollywood fever has gripped the town as season tickets have doubled. Even a Hollywood Hills style Wrexham sign now adorns a large mound as you approach the outskirts of the town. I bet Ifor and his livestock trailer business can't believe their luck.

More convincingly we have our own benefactor. The local businessman Mark Stott. The last two years have been nothing short of a revolution. The match up today involves the two biggest clubs not only in non-league but including League 2 and some of League 1. A far cry from the mid 80's when I was one of 2,000 punters rattling around Edgeley Park or in more recent years watching us drop desperately into regional non-league football. There were some high spots in between but this season maybe our best season ever along with the legendary 96/97 campaign.

We have now won twenty-two out of the last twenty-three games. I'm losing count. Today is one of the toughest tests to date. Where it wouldn't be a shock if we went out. Our Welsh hosts are on a great run themselves. Since the turn of the year they have won 12, drawn 2, lost 2. Wrexham are at home and determined to beat us. We play them again at the Racecourse in the league. It is a psychological battle as mathematically they could still catch us. We would need to blow up in a big way but the possibility is still there. Wrexham are our closest challengers and we can't take anything for granted. With only one automatic promotion place we have to secure top spot and avoid the lottery of the play-offs.

I've tried to avoid social media but sometimes it's just too tempting. Our success has brought some inevitable criticism or jealousy. So called football finance commentators on twitter have highlighted our 20/21 lockdown accounts. Including debt that has already been paid back from our infrastructure improvements. Coupled with no matchday income in the accounts period, the loss is not reflective of the current finances. The fact the update has been posted on our website in the last week meaning these so-called experts did little homework. I let them know of course.

Meanwhile on twitter the guy who owns Forest Green and others criticised our team flying to Eastleigh. Claiming we are contributing disgracefully to global warming. The fact that the ground is next to the airport, the flight was already scheduled and it was more expensive to go on the train being ignored. The team took up seats on a scheduled flight. The coach option would have contributed additional carbon as the plane was flying anyway. The ridiculous cost of the train is probably more of an issue. I let the fella from Forest Green know. A virtue signalling owner who is about to construct a new ground they don't need. He is making it out of wood apparently but must fail to realise how much carbon those massive construction vehicles spew into the atmosphere.

The drive down to the ground was quick as we sped past the Runcorn oil refineries, bypassed Chester and crossed the border into North Cymru. Early start for my teenage son Jonnie but he had just about woken up as we looked out for that Hollywood Hills Wrexham sign. Not sure whether that thing is just good fun or a tad embarrassing. After all, one nestles above Hollywood overlooking the sprawl of LA. The other is on a mound next to a duel carriageway near Wrexham.

Once inside the impressive Racecourse Ground, the Welsh/English banter was in full flow as we took our seats adjacent to Wrexham's singing section. The stadium will be Championship standard when they replace the crumbling kop which is currently covered in a massive advertising tarpaulin. The County contingent is in fine voice as we regale the Welsh folk with chants about our top of the league status. Our intentions are made clear as Challinor selects a first team line-up which includes new boy Andy Cannon. In the first half Andy is the stand-out player. The game swung when he was substituted after sixty minutes. Before that we were the better side.

County should have scored twice in the first half through Quigley. One header which may have been buried on another day, the other a shot where Scott didn't connect properly and the ball bobbled wide. Slight concern at the moment about Scott's solitary goal return in 2022. Second half the Red Dragons came out with more intent. Croasdale came on for Cannon just after the hour and we missed our new signing who had been outstanding. However, we had another golden opportunity to take the lead but Sarcevic somehow hooked the ball over the bar from three yards out.

The hosts forced a couple of outstanding saves from Hinchliffe. The game was looking like it was going to penalties when Wrexham's best player Mullin scored a superb goal lobbing the ball from outside the box over Hinchliffe and just under the bar. A killer goal scored on ninety minutes. Four minutes later in injury time that man Mullin tapped another one in to seal County's fate.

It would have been great to walk up Wembley Way but it was not to be. We were the better side but Mullin was lethal. We weren't and maybe that is a lesson learned. Challinor commented that when you play a good team matches are won on moments. Mullin delivered for the Welshmen. The Wrexham fans celebrated like they'd won the cup and league this afternoon. The table says we are eleven points clear of them and ten points clear of third place Halifax. I'm sure the boys will take this on the chin and concentrate on the league and deliver the title.

Fair play to Wrexham though. Great atmosphere, good ground, loud fans. We didn't see their Hollywood sign but I'm sure it is worth a visit.

Saturday 9th April 2022
County 5   Southend 0

It seems an age since I travelled down to the Essex coast for the first away game of the season v Southend. Since then Rusk was sacked when we were tenth in the table in late October. Challinor led us on an unprecedented winning streak which somehow took us to the top of the league in a couple of months. We then opened up an eleven-point lead. An amazing achievement by the manager and team. Slight setback last week as we bowed out of the FA Trophy in the semi-final against Wrexham and only one-step from Wembley. I thought we were going to complete a treble including the Cheshire Cup to complete a perfect season. In reality our two cup comps are easily forgettable. No one really remembers who won those two cups but I was invested in the journey. A perfect season is still achievable by securing the big prize of a return to the football league. Going up as champions would be perfection.

Today we are back to league action and I am convinced our boys will deliver. Comfort provided by the fact we are the best footballing side in the division with the best manager. We have been superb. Our opponents were in fine form after a terrible start to the season. Then recently dropped off losing four out of the last five. After climbing to the edge of the play-offs, the Shrimpers have settled in mid table with a gap that is too big to bridge for the play-off mix. You could say that our visitors are an Essex version of us. Traditional ground with a similar capacity, similar size fan base and comparable football league history. Fortunately, our financial situation is stable while the Shrimpers have an uncertain future restricting investment.

It looks like a two-horse race between us and Wrexham now. Others are drawing games but our Welsh challengers are on a winning streak. They won on Tuesday and again today. As we are kicking off at 5:20pm on the live BT Sport match we know the three o'clock results. Our Welsh challengers were

1-2 down to Eastleigh at home until they clawed it back and that man Mullin converted a pen in the ninety fifth minute to win it 3-2. Another late, late win for them which means they are only five points behind before kick-off but we have today's game in hand.

With the sun shining on a crisp day the conditions are perfect for the players and a dedication day to our legendary ex-manager Danny Bergara. The man from Uruguay that transformed us in the late eighties and early nineties. Achieving a first promotion in twenty-four years and leading us to four Wembley appearances. With the main stand already named after the great man, a statue is planned for outside the Cheadle End. Our current manager is doing well too and is on his way to historical recognition. We have surpassed the most wins in a season over-taking the twenty-four achieved by the 1966/67 Fourth Division championship campaign. If we win today we match our maximum amount of points in a season and I've lost track of the most wins in a certain amount of matches achievements.

Another bumper crowd of 7,738 includes 371 Shrimpers fans. Considering they aren't going up or down that is a great effort all the way from Southend and back. Hats off to the level of chanting too. Adjacent to us in the Pop Side you could hear them all match even as our goals went in and right until the ninetieth minute. There were five goals to the Shrimpers zero which make their support even more impressive.

Our crowd was impressive too with the volume. You would expect that as we've been bang in form for six months. Today's performance ranks as one of the best since Challinor took over. Our opposition weren't great but we just calmly took them apart. Uber professional. Watching the match back on telly, the commentators and pundits purred with compliments saying that we look good enough to go for another promotion next year. Let's not get too carried away though, there are still eight games to go. Wrexham look like they are going to push us all the way but after today's victory we have retained that precious eight-point gap plus a much better goal difference as insurance.

All the goals were quality. The first one by Collar (a tap in from five yards after a nice move and scramble in the box) was followed by a lovely driven shot by Hippolyte from just outside the Shrimpers eighteen-yard box. A Paddy Madden brace after the interval doubled the score line before substitute Andy Cannon completed the rout late on. Madden's first was a peach of a volley from just inside the box and his second a simple header at the back post. New boy Cannon came on and converted a nice free kick through a poorly arranged Southend wall. The Shrimpers were defensively generous but we still had to convert the chances.

An impressive performance by Quigs earned him the deserved man of the match prize. Scott has struggled to score since the turn of the year but he adds so much to the team. A nuisance factor that creates space and provides assists. Big, determined and with a team ethic and work rate that any young footballer should study. He is the definition of team player. Another brilliant team player is Paddy Madden. A centre forward that converts chances one minute then defends deep the next. Paddy is the top candidate for player of the year.

Another great performance under a bit of pressure with Wrexham's two wins this week. We came through with flying colours in a relentless run of results that makes us strong favourites to win the league. More great support from the County fans with many dressed in classic retro shirts from the Danny Bergara era in tribute to the great man. Next stop a trip to Cleethorpes and a visit to the home of fishfingers and Grimsby Town.

Friday 15th April 2022
Grimsby 2   County 1

Nice Good Friday visit to sunny Cleethorpes. The seaside town is the location for our hosts which is connected to Grimsby. I've never been. I know it's a fishing town. It's where most kids fishfingers have come from for generations. The seaside bit is probably like a mini-Blackpool. I wouldn't go as far as to say our destination is an east coast English Riviera but it has been good enough for English holidaymakers through the ages. Since the trend for foreign package holiday's Cleethorpes glory days are over but I'll reserve judgement until I have seen it. For some this will be an overnight stay and all-day drinking session. For me it is a trip with my eldest son back from Uni. So a few beers for him but with me as the chauffeur.

Not to worry as I'll make up for it this bank holiday weekend. County are on the up and so is the town. In recent years there's been a resurrection of sorts. New bars on the market, trendy gin houses on Underbank. A Michelin green star restaurant. Even a French restaurant in the refurbished Winters site at Underbank. Bistro Marc opens soon. A school friend of Kath's returns to her hometown with her French-Canadian chef husband. Bloomin eck we're on the up.

It is great to share the awaydays with my lads and another 1,400 County fans today. These are our salad days. I might not be as youthful as I once was but I'm certainly carefree. Having my football team winning so regularly is a bonus. Might as well enjoy this run as much as possible. One thing is for sure in football, it will all end at some point. Probably when we are in the Championship and hover above the relegation zone. I trust in Stott and his six-year plan to get us to the penultimate level in football. The second tier and to mix it with the big boys in the Championship. It's still on. Promotion this year and then two more in the next three. No problem.

I've had to do a bit of research on how to get to our sunny seaside destination. I know it is somewhere under Hull on the east coast. Unlike Kings Lynn which involved an A road schlep across Woodhead and the Lincolnshire plains, Grimsby looks like motorways all the way and doable within two hours. Across the M62, down the M18 for a bit then cross country on the M180. I've never been to the end of the M180, probably the only motorway in the country I haven't done the full length of. You do need a really good reason to fully transverse it though. The only towns on it are Scunthorpe and Grimsby.

We've left early to make sure we have time for a pre-match pint and to park somewhere near the ground. Apparently Blundell Park (also known as Cleethorpes Stadium) is near the top of the worst stadiums to park near league. Hemmed in by terraced houses the ground is a traditional football ground with four different stands and a bit of character. With a 10,000 capacity so similar to Edgeley Park. It went all seater in 1995 reducing its capacity down from 27,000. That's a shame. The Mariners have had 32,000 in there versus Wolves in 1937. When County redevelop the Pop Side I hope they have some safe standing in there.

A relatively easy journey over was enjoyed until the last few miles when a ridiculous 40mph speed limit is imposed for no apparent reason on the M180. No evidence of any planned road works. Maybe implemented to slow you down as there is no rush to get to Grimsby as there is nothing there. The River Humber is lined with factories and oil refineries on the way in and once there you can see massive fish processing plants. Also what looked like a new super-sized fish factory ship. A daunting edifice and something that depressingly probably dredges the bottom of the sea in an industrial process disturbing the ecosystem in the process.

The sun is shining and Kath has decided to join us for the run out. The plan is she will find a nice bit of the Cleethorpes sea front and sit in the sun with her easel drawing a seaside scene. Reporting back after the match Kath said that the sea front was nicer than expected in the sun but there is a proliferation of low budget arcades and fish and chip shops. The pier has been chopped off halfway down and the only vendors left are you guessed it, a fish and chip kiosk.

Approaching the away stand, the whole façade is covered in ship-lapped wood. I thought timber was banned from football grounds. Maybe it is just banned from the inside. Inside there is a nice old school bar. A room that looks like it has been the same for decades. Murals on the wall depict Gordon Banks and Bobby Moore circa 1966 and players from the early 90's. We get a quick pint from the selection of Carling or Carling. Fortunately, it was very cold to make it palatable. The away end is bouncing. There are a couple of massive flags being waved and blue smoke bombs going off. The first half sees a relentless show of support from the Hatters fans with the home fans looking particularly impressed with our support. The team are impressive too looking a league above our hosts. The Mariners are chasing shadows. It took only thirteen minutes to take the lead. Quigley got a much needed first goal for two months rolling in a flick on from Madden.

With County creating chances and looking on the way to another three point the referee intervened to stunt our progress. Sarcevic went in high for a challenge slightly late and was punished with a straight red ten minutes before half-time. The Grimsby player stayed down as is if he had been shot before miraculously recovering. A challenge that probably didn't need to be attempted. County still continued to dominate and the feeling was that we could see the second half out even with ten men.

In reality it is rare that a team goes a whole half of football with ten men and wins. In the second period The Mariners came into the match moving the ball around well to try and tire us out. After sixty-four minutes McAtee cut in from the right and slotted past Hinchliffe. If we could have held out for another ten minutes we probably would have secured at least a point. Twelve minutes later our hosts scored again from a corner to take the lead. The Grimsby fans loved it and started to give us some stick. Very quiet in the first half, the home fans came to life and the rest of the match was an exchange of banter. The County fans never stopped their support for the team though.

With points in the bag the County fans took this defeat on the chin, singing to the end with the players applauding us at the final whistle. They seemed genuinely in awe of our support. Post-match many home fans said that we were the best away fans they had seen at Blundell Park. Wrexham and Halifax only drew so this defeat was not as bad as it may have been with us still having a seven-point gap at the top.

We collected Kath at our rendezvous point and sped away from Cleethorpes/Grimsby back towards civilisation. A lovely sunny day and a really enjoyable match even in defeat. Without the sending off we would have won that match. The players fought bravely with ten men and everything still bodes well for the run in.

Monday 18th April 2022
County 1   Solihull Moors 0

Two games in four days with this Easter Bank Holiday Monday match against our Brummie visitors who are challenging for a top three place in the league. Another tough match with The Moors being one of the form teams in the league with only one defeat in fourteen matches. With our first defeat since December on Friday softened by Wrexham and Halifax only drawing, we have a seven-point lead over second place Wrexham. Halifax lie in third, eight points behind having played an extra game. Today's visitors are fourth ten points behind us and we have a game in hand on them.

Moors will be looking for another upset by earning points from this match as they try to secure a top three place. Top three means you go straight to the play-off semi-final rather than play an extra match if you finish fourth to seventh. So, we are definitely at the business end of the season. Sarcevic is out due to his red card at Grimsby. Another pleasant spring day greets us at a sold-out Edgeley Park. The home sections are completely sold out. The Moors fans have been moved into the Railway End and we have all of the Pop Side. The attendance is a bumper 9,200.

Cannon comes in for the suspended Sarcevic. The rest is pretty much unchanged from our visit to Cleethorpes. Moors are well organised tough and dangerous on the break. Their number 11 has a brief to follow Cannon wherever he goes. He is man marking so tight he'll probably follow Cannon home after the match. This effectively cancels out our new midfielder leaving Croasdale as the main playmaker in the first half. Their danger man Dallas had a couple of first half chances. Their tackling was fierce with three borderline red card assaults in the match. The ref was lenient handing out three yellows.

In the second half Rydel was tripped in the box but Madden missed the penalty. A critical point in what is a tight match where one goal is likely to decide it. To be fair Solihull are one of the best teams we've played this year albeit industrial tacklers. With the game looking like a 0-0, Challinor made typically successful subs. Hippolyte, Crankshaw and Jennings came on to good effect. Moors also mixed it up bringing on a six foot eleven forward to go long in the final minutes. Could we force a goal? In injury time Hippolyte supplied that man Madden who poked home from close range. The roof came off the Pop Side, Cheadle End and Main Stand. A massive three points against one of the best teams desperate for the points themselves.

With Wrexham winning again this was a key point in the run in. We maintain the seven-point gap with six games to go. If it was down to four or five points it would be too close for comfort. Still work to be done but the super Hatters are putting a massive shift in. We are on course. 9,200 fans went home happy with a late, late winner raising the roof. A visceral moment. Celebration mixed with relief, mixed with unbridled joy. A pure football moment. There are hundreds if not thousands of new fans in the making. Hopefully, they come back for more County excitement. Next stop cider country.

Saturday 23rd April 2022
Yeovil 2   County 1

We travel to Somerset to play the beleaguered Glovers in a garment themed contest against the Hatters from Stockport. Our hosts are safely sat in mid-table but the general atmosphere around the club is not good. With only one player under contract past the end of the season they recently lost their manager to Woking. A contract was offered for next season to Darren Sarll, something Glovers chairman and owner Scott Priestnall couldn't guaranty. In another dodgy football takeover the club has been plunged into further debt after Priestnall took out a large loan from Sport England to pay off the HMRC for outstanding tax arrears.

It all sounds familiar to us of course. On and off the pitch as Yeovil made it all the way to the Championship as recently as 2012/13. One season was spent with the big boys before s drop back down the divisions into The National League in 2018. Originally called Yeovil & Petters United, the Glovers are a traditional old non-league team with their debut in the Football league being as recent 2004. Today fortunes have changes for both teams. While our hosts are in the midst of uncertainty we have had our revolution in recent seasons.

An interesting historical moment for the Glovers is their 1948/49 FA Cup run. A record 17,000 Yeovil fans filled the old Huish Park to witness a 2-1 victory over Sunderland in the fourth round. They were defeated 8–0 in the following round by Manchester United. 6,000 Glovers fans travelled to Maine Road, United's temporary home and formed part of a mammoth 81,000 crowd. 800 County fans have travelled today to the new Huish Park. The new ground was opened in 1990 and is built on an old army camp.

It was after the Woking away match earlier this season that I last travelled to these parts with work. I passed the massive Thatcher's cider factory. The edifice nestles unexpectedly in a village not far from Yeovil and is a big local employer and sponsor of Yeovil FC. As if the football club didn't have enough problems the famous Thatcher's cider have also been under attack from the Countering Coulston organisation a Bristol based anti-slavery group. Thatcher's are a members of the Society of Merchant Venturers (SMV). A group that originally had links to the slave trade. A Boycott Thatcher's campaign started before the beleaguered cider makers proved that they have only been members for ten years and the SMV are now a forward thinking corporately responsible entity.

So after all the trials and tribulations in these parts and Covid, Ukraine and inflation it is with some relief that I travel in the knowledge that at least County are on a sound footing. Last week's last-minute winner at home to Solihull was a key win. It feels like we are on our way now. Wrexham have pushed us hard but that last minute winner was something champions pull out of the hat. The journey is about four hours unless you stop for more than a comfort break. I did it in just under four hours without any traffic hold ups. I went past this destination on the way to Weymouth. Today's trip is probably my third longest County journey this season after Weymouth and Southend. I've racked up nearly 6,000 miles this season following the Hatters so far according to an app on my phone.

All this mileage has been well worth the effort though. What a season and what a team. I'm in the seats and the rest of the travelling County army are to my right behind the goal on the open terrace. There has been a carnival atmosphere for a while now. Challinor's men have been top of the league since the 25th January. When we lost 0-3 at home to Yeovil on 11th September we were sixteenth. That was during the underwhelming regime of McGhee and Rusk. That duo are now doing an even more underwhelming job at Dundee. McGhee seems to have completely lost the plot claiming he isn't going to eat and sleep all week so he can concentrate on the next match. Or go naked for a week if they lose!

The Glovers run on in their traditional green shirts which is almost a unique look. Maybe along with Plymouth and possibly Forest Green but I don't really count them as a proper club. They're sort of a virtuous version of Salford City. Their owner being a bit annoying, bank rolling them while selling his renewable energy and vegan pies. I'm slightly merry after a couple of pints of Thatcher's. I've had a pie (a real meat one) to absorb the beverage and will have another snack at half time to ensure my equilibrium is suitable for the return journey. County are in our home colours of all blue.

The first half lacked any equilibrium from County as pretty much all of our players had an off day. The fans kept singing but the players couldn't get it together. Without any notable chances from the Hatters, Yeovil must have wondered what all the fuss about us is. So much so they decided to take the lead just before half time. Subs were made at the break with Hippolyte and Crankshaw entering the fray. I expected us to come out all guns blazing but we fired blanks for the first ten minutes. Then Neufville strides through and slots past Hinchliffe. 0-2 and a shocker.

With twenty minutes to play County finally scored as Hippolyte drove home. But immediately Collar is harshly sent off for a high foot. It is a red but unintentionally high by our midfielder. Shocker and a three-match ban. Even the 800 loyal Hatters fans have gone quiet. They stayed with the players in a turgid first half but the wind has been taken out of their sails. This is a poor performance and we are now down to ten men. A huge fifteen minutes remain. The impressive County fans turn up the volume again to try and push the players on. This is a strange situation for the team and the fans after such an impressive run since November.

The game peters out as Yeovil complete the double over us this season. We put the pressure on in the last five minutes but to no avail. Are they a bogey team? Is this a one-off poor display? I hope so. With Sarcevic and Collar now on a suspension they have probably booked themselves a place in the Cheshire Cup final on Tuesday as the three-match bans don't count. Wrexham play later today on TV and twice more before our late kick-off next Saturday against Boreham Wood. We have opened the door to Wrexham but it's still in our hands.

Hopefully just a hiccup. It's a long way back to Cheshire from Somerset. It's been rare to travel back after defeat in the last six months. Can't complain too much and I'm confident County will be back with a bang.

NB- later on Wrexham kicked off at 5:20pm. The Red Dragons scored from a jammy heavily deflected shot just on half time. It looked nailed on that our challengers would bag three points reducing our lead to four points. Woking weren't perturbed and under the influence of Yeovil's ex-manager Darren Sarll dug out a 2-1 victory. The return journey was transformed with Woking's second goal. Somewhere around Droitwich the mood turned to celebration. The seven-point gap is maintained and we have a better goal difference of ten goals.

Saturday 26th April 2022
Cheshire Senior Cup Final
County 5   Vauxhall Motors 0

A cup final at EP and an opportunity to do a double of sorts. This is such a minor competition that a lot of County followers haven't bothered with it. But as it is a final we should get a decent crowd in tonight. I have been to every match in this comp in a show of loyalty and interest in seeing our fringe players and impressive youth players. Cody Johnson for example emerged in the competition this season. Probably the most promising County youngster I have ever seen. In truth I was motivated to attend some of the early rounds of this cup because I am writing this book. Especially the Macclesfield away tie when I was feeling rough and had to stand on an open terrace getting the most pissed wet through I've ever been.

It has all been worth it this season. Since Challinor took over as manager we have been really good in pretty much every match. In fact we've won probably 98% of them. What a record and what a season. Tonight the opposition are a team named after a car factory in Ellesmere Port. It will be nice to play them as we progress towards a possible league title and return to the Football League. Last time we played them was in a league match as a part time team in regional non-league football. I'm not going to check our record but I do remember beating them 4-1 at EP and a losing to them at their place. A defeat in a period when our current position would seem impossible. I recall one of my lads played a competition there the same week. The venue being a sports complex where Vauxhall Motors pitch was surrounded by railings with just one proper stand. Proper non-league.

Fair play to our automotive monikered opponents. They beat Runcorn on pens in the semi, Tranmere in the quarters and 1874 Northwich before that. Northwich being probably the smallest town to have three teams. Northwich Vics, 1874 and Witton. Just thought I'd throw that in to demonstrate non-league knowledge. Tonight will be one of Vauxhall's biggest matches in their history and possibly the biggest crowd they will have played to. The Motormen's record home attendance is 1,752 versus Chester in 2012. As far as quality goes they are a Vauxhall Astra diesel and we are a 32-valve Calibra. Apologies if that line is lost on anyone. You probably need to be over forty to remember those car models.

A couple of thousand fans turn up with 128 from Ellesmere Port. A good number being friends and family of the Vauxhall Motors players. The crowd is quite a bit lower than the semi against Crewe probably due to the fact we have three games this week. The Motormen enter the pitch in all fluorescent yellow looking like an advert for PPE or those yellow vests worn on building sites. County are in all blue with eleven changes from the last match at Yeovil. All the players have seen first team league action apart from the impressive Cody Johnson and Scott Holding. Johnson was man of the match too. Cody has just earned himself a professional contract in recognition of his performances in the cups and to deter any other teams from nicking him.

Our opponents are into industrial tackling and the referee is turning a blind eye. Reid cops a hand in the face and goes down theatrically before making a miraculous recovery and receiving the wrath of their defenders. Newby cops it too as he pushes the ball down the wings. Cody Johnson is too smart and quick anticipating the challenges. What a prospect. Sarcevic is the first player in the referee's book though with a rash challenge. He's serving a ban in the league for a similar indiscretion.

Reid finally registered reward for our first half domination with a neat, flicked header after forty minutes. He did a typically cocky celebration in front of the Vauxhall fans. The biggest cheer is for the news that Weymouth have gone one up against Wrexham but the Red Dragons came back in the second half winning 6-1. Our second half is one way traffic. Within two minutes Jennings volleyed in. Twenty minutes later Newby drilled a low shot home. Jennings got his brace with fifteen minutes left from another low drive albeit deflected in by a defender. Then just near the end Newby delivered a lovely chip that was nodded in by Duffus to make it five.

Sat in the Main Stand the temperature dramatically dropped near the end. With just my County sweatshirt on I was ready to get back into the warm and fortunately the presentation ceremony was pretty quick. The old bods from the Cheshire FA looked a bit unsure of the procedure but eventually our opponents took the initiative and collected their medals from a table set up in front of the tunnel. The County lads then looked a bit confused about who should go first before Reid shoved our young defender Scott Holding forward. Captain Keane lifted the cup to the delight of the Main Stand before jogging over to the Cheadle End to show off the silverware.

It was a nice moment to see County lift silverware. We won this cup in 2016 and the National League North trophy in 2019. Before that you had to go back to 1967 and our Fourth Division champions season for actual silverware. We've had lots of promotions and Wembley appearances but in terms of cups this is the haul. I saw some old-time fans looking really chuffed with the cup. The youngsters loved it too. Maybe not an important bit of silverware but worth having and worth attending the match for. Now let's get promoted.

Saturday 30th April 2022
County 1   Boreham Wood 2

I've been lucky with fixture clash avoidance in pursuit of writing this blog. Today's match was moved to a 5:20pm kick off for TV meaning that I can attend my youngest son Jonnie's cup final at 2pm. Watching all a team's matches in a given season amounts to about sixty or more games. If you've got a wife, kids, full time job and other social activity opps it is almost impossible to not get into fixture clashes. Luckily, I've avoided any weddings, funerals or unavoidable family reunions and graduations etc. I've body-swerved any life-threatening injuries, match threatening illness or force majeure. I've missed one or two matches through choice. Such as Dover away when I'd travelled to Newcastle and back the day before and to go to the other end of the country and back the next day was a motorway too far.

The cup final venue for Jonnie's match is West Didsbury & Chorlton's Brookburn Rd in leafy Chorltonville. A lovely ground with a great club house. Home to the Wests ultra's, Chorlton's bohemian fan group. Akin to a mini–St Pauli FC, Hamburg's left leaning football club. They have a small stand they call the Curva Shed which is covered in brilliant football stickers. Mostly with a left-wing sentiment. Wests have just been promoted to the Northwest Counties Premier Division with impressive crowds of around 450 and up to 800. I'm into a bit of ground hopping and have even considered writing a book about all the teams in Greater Manchester.

The GM region has a mind boggling thirty-eight established clubs in the top ten leagues. The top ten leagues partake in the FA Cup starting in August each year. That is Man Utd and City all the way down to the likes of Cheadle Town, Prestwich Heys and Wests. The closest team to my house looks like Cheadle Town at 1.8 miles, then probably Wythenshawe Amateurs, County and West Didsbury etc. A visit to all thirty-eight teams for a match in a given season might make a decent read. If you are into that kind of thing.

The other aspect of our 5:20 kick off is that Wrexham have already completed their 3pm kick-off. Meaning we have two games in hand on them. They came back to defeat

Weymouth 6-1 mid-week and this afternoon managed a 1-0 win at home to Sarfend. One point behind but we have those two games in hand. Jonnie's team, meanwhile, go one nil up , three one down before winning 5-3 and lifting the cup. Cracking match. Wests secretary informs me that they had 2,000 in for their final match of the season versus Alsager. Even more impressive than my attendance recollections.

Back at EP, the Wrexham victory has injected a bit of pre-match nerves. We are in control of our destiny mathematically but it depends on whether our opposition care. Obviously, they don't and the Wood decide to score the first goal after about twenty minutes. It was a gift as Palmer let a back pass go under his foot and one of their forwards slotted home. County come back and pepper the Boreham Wood goal forcing a couple of good saves from their keeper. Dave Challinor was interviewed in a national newspaper this week. When he took over we were tenth and he said at the time that the play-offs would be a result. Top three would be brilliant. We are top.

Rydel just misses the top right-hand corner of Woods net as the ref blows his whistle. County go in 0-1 at half time and we are hoping for a typically positive half time team talk. DC is good at the half time break. His calm persona presumably creating a controlled analysis. The lads have been good in the first half without pulling up trees. A champions level second half effort is required. Seven minutes in DC decides on changes and brings on Crankshaw and Cannon.

Unfortunately, the Wood score a second. A loose ball hooked over Hinchliffe. The visiting fans are in the uncovered Railway End wearing sou'westers. It is warm and there have been a couple of drops of rain. Presumably, they've never been north of Watford and have researched survival equipment for travel to the provinces. There are only 44 of them in the 8,878 crowd. You literally could fit them into a large minibus. Oldham have this to look forward to next season now they've been relegated. Some large away followings and some miniscule non-league followings.

We huffed and puffed. For all our effort we didn't threaten the resolute defence enough until the last minute when Newby forced the ball home from close range. Hippolyte agonisingly hit the post in the last seconds. County missed Collar and Sarcevic today. We had enough to win the game but the visitors played well and took their chances. It just didn't quite click. Sarcevic is back for the next match. Seventeen matches without defeat at Edgeley Park came to an end. A rare disappointing day for County which will give Wrexham hope that they can pull it back and catch us. Our destiny is in our hands still. Fair play to Boreham Wood. We go again on Monday away at Chesterfield.

Some County fans have been panicking on social media and over critical. We have lost three in four in the league after an amazing record-breaking undefeated run. Rather than going completely off the boil, sending offs have hit us. A first half sending off at Grimsby when we were in control and playing well. Then another sending off at Torquay in a game we probably would have got at least a point from. Both sending offs were a tad harsh. So luck has gone against us. But we've probably had luck elsewhere. A football season is a long journey of twists and turns. I'm still confident. Maybe it is my vintage that provides a level-headed optimism.

CHAPTER TEN
May 2022

Monday 2nd May 2022
Chesterfield 0   County 1

Saturday's defeat has fully sunk in. Wrexham will be boosted by our recent dip in form. However, they play our opponents on Saturday, Boreham Wood away today. A decent side who have a resolute defensive style limiting all their opponents to a maximum two goals this season at their ground. They've only conceded two twice at home. This statistical "analysis" suggests that if Wrexham concede today they will need to play really well to win. There you go, as I've said before, my glass is always half full.

More importantly, Dave Challinor will be telling our heroes to forget about our challengers and just win our games. If we do, we win the league. Of course it isn't that simple and as Alex Ferguson once said it is squeaky bum time. Fortunately, DC is a calm, experienced manager who has won promotion several times before with Colwyn Bay, Fylde and Hartlepool. Trust in Dave. Hold our nerves, play our game, keep the team spirit going, keep calm and carry on.

With a magical Chesterfield ticket in my wallet ready for the match, I prepare to embark on one of my favourite awayday excursions. Almost immediately after leaving Stockport, you enter the Peak District. Lovely and probably an area of outstanding beauty. I haven't checked but it must be. Past Chapel-en-le Frith, Tideswell, Eyam, Baslow and eventually into the town with a crooked spire. I've more than likely driven or ridden every road in the Peak District over the years. Being a biker, this area is a natural destination for a blast.

I have watched County a few times at Chesterfield at their old Saltergate ground. A wonderfully traditional but dilapidated stadium forever etched in Hatters history after we won promotion there in 96/97. Probably our greatest ever season. Interestingly I checked and our average home attendance that season was 6,424. This season it is over 6,800 which is brilliant considering we are in the National League. The new Chesterfield ground is typical of new ones. I could go on for ages and sound like a boring old traditionalist, but I'll be brief.

The new ground is called the Technique Stadium formerly the B2net and Proact stadium. Hopefully, ours will always be called Edgeley Park. The Technique (presumably some type of shop or gym sponsorship) nestles unimpressively between a Tesco, Aldi and a bathroom megastore on a retail park. Outside the structure is breeze block walls with blue cladding. While Rotherham has the look of a big Argos, this one has the look of a big Carphone Warehouse. Not sure if Carphone Warehouse still exists but you get the idea. Fortunately, these identikit grounds look better from the inside. The Technique is a modern 10,500 capacity ground and the blue seats and stands look ok from the inside. But for someone of my vintage there was more excitement entering a town and seeing the old-style spotlights and characterful higgledy-piggledy stands.

Getting a ticket for this match wasn't really a challenge. We have a 2,600 sold out allocation. So enough for season ticket holders plus others. This will make for a great atmosphere. Driving over I fully freshened up as a slight hangover wore off after a bank holiday night out. We have filled a full stand behind the goal and about a quarter of an adjacent stand. I am pretty positive but nervous at the same time. Nerves develop as the kick-off approaches. Banter is lively but nervous. The lady sat to my left is bricking it. It really is crunch time.

Can Boreham Wood do us a favour at home to Wrexham? We have four changes as Quigs drops to the bench with a slight muscle pull and is replaced by Duffus who makes his first start. Keano comes in for Hogan, Cannon starts and Sarcevic returns after suspension. Nerves jingle but County calm me down as we make a bright start. We look controlled while Chesterfield appear off the pace, hit by injuries and out of form. Ex-County player and Spireites boss Paul Cook goes apoplectic after a refs decision and gets a yellow card. The Hatters fans provide a rendition of "Paul Cook is a County fan."

Cook's mood wouldn't have improved after thirty-four minutes when the ref gave us a pen. Chesterfield defender Calvin Miller clearly handled the ball on the edge of the box. The fourth official made the decision. Looking back on the TV footage it was definitely in the box in my opinion. Madden dispatched the pen into the back of the net and the County fans went wild. Just before half time County produced a lovely move with the impressive Duffus turning and chipping the keeper but the ball bounced off the crossbar.

Second half saw an improvement from our hosts with the annoying, tall and disruptive Tom Denton causing a few problems. Their sub-Asante looked lively up front without threatening our goal and Cook will have been disappointed with his team's performance. Meanwhile at Boreham Wood ex-Wrexham player Fyfield was sent off for The Wood in the first half and top scorer Mullin converted again for our challengers just after half-time. As the game concluded in Derbyshire it looked like we had gained a precious three points but that Wrexham were still hunting us down. Fortunately, Boreham Wood converted a penalty in the eighty-ninth minute. The county fans went wild again.

We've been a bit out of luck in recent matches but maybe the luck evened itself out today. With Boreham Wood down to ten men after forty minutes it was likely that Wrexham would go on to win. But a last-minute pen pulled them back to give County an extra two points gap in the league table. At the Technique there was a great atmosphere, a 9,200 crowd and a great advert for the National league. The County fans were loud and proud. At the end, the players came over to celebrate and we could be champions with a victory at Wrexham this coming Sunday. If not, we still have two home games to finish the season and hopefully get the points we need.

Sunday 8th May 2022
Wrexham 3   County 0

Lady luck shone her magic beams upon me for this one. I eventually secured a ticket. They are like gold dust as demand outstripped supply. Only 1,200 tickets were made available to County fans and we have approx. 2,800 season ticket holders. Demand would have been for up to 5,000 tickets such is the excitement for the conclusion to our season. When they went on sale I had a hopeless go at navigating the online ticket system before rushing down to the ground to queue with other season ticket holders. As the queue dissipated I was frustratingly within ten people of the ticket window before the dreaded announcement of sold out!

Rumours are that half season ticket holders managed to connect themselves to a full season tickets online. Names were taken by the ticket office manager with a promise that they would contact us full fat season tickets holders to re-allocate the tickets. I never got a call but a follow up with the ticket office came off and the golden ticket was secured.

We've been to the Racecourse recently for the FA Trophy semi-final so the journey is familiar across the border into Cymru. At the semi-final Jonnie and I were right next to the Wrexham fans in the section which contains their "nutters." This match is probably the biggest ever game in the National League for decades. We can win the league with a win today. That thought fills me with joy but also slight worry that it could kick off. Our fans have to stay off the pitch if we win otherwise the danger is that the Welsh fans will enter the fray too. Judging by some of the Wrexham fans at the semi this is a possibility. One old fat bloke rather comically spent the whole match watching the County fans and inviting them for a fight. While some of his cohorts seemed happy to join him.

Fingers-crossed we get a fair contest and no aggro. In some ways it would be nice to draw today and bag the promotion at one of the two remaining matches, both at home. Or maybe even better if would be just win it today. Or maybe we'll blow it. It really is not over yet. Mathematically the permutations have been bouncing around my cranium all week. At this stage we are more than likely going to win it unless we lose the remaining three games and Wrexham win their last two. We can win with four points from the last three games even if the Red Dragons win their two. I think it's better to just take it one game at a time.

It would have been a real shocker if I hadn't secured a ticket for today. After all the effort and away games at Nantwich and Macc in the Cheshire Cup. Not to mention all those long distant southern away trips. In the rain midweek at Bromley. In the rain at Weymouth. Midweek at Kings Lynn.

Hungover at Wealdstone. Bored senseless at Boreham Wood. Solo to Southend. Midweek at Maidenhead. Not to mention disappointed at Halifax and disillusioned at Notts County. Those last two were under Rusk. Bored at Boreham Wood was under Rusk too. The Challinor revolution games have all been worth it.

So, here we are on a Sunday lunchtime in sunny Wales. Well, the sun is breaking through the crowds. The future is bright, the future is County. Let's do it lads. The County fans are in fine voice again. Chesterfield was an amazing atmosphere. Bolton home and away and Rotherham away are also vying for top spot in the best atmosphere of the season table. The next two home matches will be special. In fact the whole season has been special. The fans have been brilliant. Today could top it though. If we win, the noise will rattle the bolts loose in the stanchions and roof of this stand.

The noise is already rattling the bolts from both sets of fans pre-kick-off. I've got to give credit to the Wrexham fans and the volume they create. We were loud too and our team quietened the home fans down in the first twenty-five minutes. County looked controlled and created chances but couldn't convert. Sarcevic and Madden had good opportunities. The rest of the match could be described as wretched in Wrexham. The home side did a number on us by breaking on the counter taking their chances. County meanwhile spawned chances with the usually reliable Madden squandering a couple more in the second half. The referee didn't help by having a policy of letting players off and not giving fouls. He created a rod for his own back by not getting his card out then having to let things go. On balance to the advantage of the home side.

Wrexham scored their first just after half an hour from a header at the near post from a throw-in. County couldn't be faulted for effort but were hit by the killer blow of a second goal right on half time. Mullin was played through from the halfway line and made no mistake by slotting past

Hinchliffe. We were the better side overall but Wrexham took their chances.

Second half, the Red Dragons looked energised and the home crowd got behind them from all of their three stands. Ollie Palmer glanced in a header for his brace at the start of the second half. Two killer goals either side of half time meant we had a mammoth task against a good side. County didn't look convincing in the second period with several unforced errors. Madden could and should have scored with a stooping header. It just wasn't his day. Paddy has been immense this season so we can forgive him. A deflated away end struggled to muster many chants in the second half. There was a massive expectation of potentially winning the league this afternoon so it was understandable considering we were three down after forty-six minutes.

The permutations were talked about after the third goal. With any points unlikely the second half was spent chatting about the possible outcomes. Simply put we need four points from the last two games as we can't expect Wrexham to drop points. As the final whistle blew I got an early dart to the car. No point getting trapped in the one-way out car park behind the away stand after such a deflating afternoon. Our fans kept supporting the team in the face of relentless banter from the Welsh crowd in the second half. A few left early. I always wait for the final whistle but made a quick escape. It could have been a joyous celebration. However, maybe in the end, it will be better to do it at Edgeley Park.

My thoughts post-match stay positive considering our advantage over Wrexham in terms of it being in our own hands. I also concluded that this is typical County. We are good enough to have already won this league. Somehow, a few red cards and missed chances in front of goal recently have conspired to make this the nail-biter it wasn't supposed to be. It is still in our hands but we still need a win and a draw. It's not over until the fat lady sings. I hope that when she finally sings, she's singing our song.

Wednesday 11th May 2022
County 1   Torquay United 0

Dave Challinor came out after the Wrexham match with his first interview critical about the players. After other recent defeats he has been very supportive. We've been unlucky with a couple of soft red cards. Especially at Grimsby in a game we would have won with eleven men. The effort has always been there but concentration and some discipline has gone missing. After Wrexham Dave was critical of our back three and to be fair Palmer and Hogan have made mistakes recently leading to goals. Also, Quigs came in for criticism. DC stating that although Scott is a great lad and grafter, instructions were for him to ensure the ball sticks with him and to keep possession. To be fair, Quigs goal return has been low recently and the ball does escape him too much.

The message to the players for this match tonight is the same as at the Racecourse. Show character, rise to the challenge and handle the pressure. This includes taking your chances. Madden for example has been great this season but at the crunch moments at Wrexham he failed to convert any of four good chances. Meanwhile for Wrexham Mullin and Palmer were deadly strikers. We are better than Wrexham as a footballing team but they have the best strikers. That is the crux of the matter at the sharp end of the season. Tonight is an opportunity to control our own destiny and that requires goals to win matches. Our recent goal return has faded compared to earlier in the season.

The fans are doing their part. Another big crowd and another fans march pre-match. These marches have been brilliant with flares, flags, banners and hundreds of fans singing through the streets on the way to the ground and into the stadium. The players need to take their chances. For all our possession our goal return has been low recently. Unfortunately, it looks like the impressive Duffus has a serious injury and will not be an option now. So it is down to Madden and in particular Quigley to start to take chances and bag some goals. The only other forward option is Jennings. Fortunately, Collar is back tonight to offer a goal threat from midfield.

Jonnie and I are in confident mood. With two home matches we are sure the home crowd will help to suck the ball into the opponents net. Being a County fanatic my player analysis is totally biased. I am definitely a glass half full man. Jonnie on the other hand has a younger more realistic perspective. Maybe it's all those hours spent playing FIFA but youngsters seem to have a more analytical view. All his observations have been fairly accurate this season. He likes Palmer but doesn't believe he is one for the next couple of seasons. Hogan has a mistake in him. Quigs goes down too easy for a big man and won't score enough. I thought he was too critical earlier in the season but he may have a point.

Tonight is a chance for redemption for one or two players. Focus and victory. Play to our capabilities. I have faith. The ground is full on all four sides with County supporters as the club has opened up the Railway End to home fans. There will only be about 100 Gulls fans with their season over as they sit in midtable. So they can be accommodated at the end of the Pop Side. This means we have fans behind both goals which will hopefully assist us in scoring goals at both ends. The attendance is 9,400. Even if we fall short this season there will be some consolation in the re-birth of support for the Hatters. We have always had a loyal hardcore even in the dark days but these levels of support are unprecedented at this level.

Pre-match Jonnie and I join the march as it progresses down Castle Street. Blue flares fill the air and flags wave as the fans go through the County song book. Onlookers line the streets and stand outside the pubs. Parents wheel babies in prams, old-timers wave, youngsters jump up and down. It really is a community effort in support of the Hatters. As the march switches back for another run-down Castle Street we tail off for a pint behind the Pop Side. Seventeen-year-old

Jonnie enjoys his pint before we get in our seats and watch the ground fill up. Regulars talk excitedly with new faces around us. This season has seen the Pop Side full on several occasions which is great to be part of.

The nerves are jangling. Fingers are crossed. Positivity fills the air as the fans chant loud and proud. We are the twelfth man. I'm confident as we have the midfield strength and creativity back with the combo of Sarcevic, Collar, Cannon and Croasdale. Quigs makes way and drops to the bench. Hogan also drops to the bench with Keane, Palmer and Francis-Angol coming in to form a back three. This all makes sense for this game. What we didn't expect was that a decent Torquay side would play like they were in the play-off final. With nothing to play for, no favours were given and they put in a professional performance.

As an overview, every County fan will be proud of the boys tonight. Under what must have been intense pressure, the players put in one of their best performances of the season. When the chips were down, the players stepped up to the plate and proved that they are indeed, the best team in the league. Whatever happens against Halifax in the last game we can be happy that these lads have put in a massive effort this season. They understand what County is about and genuinely wear the shirt with pride. It was a 1-0 win but could have been 5-0. Somehow the ball wouldn't go into the net with a combination of worldy saves from their keeper and near misses. Wrexham can have no complaints about the Gulls efforts.

As mentioned in the last book and previously in this story, I've been putting my lads through County conversion therapy for years. As both are United sympathisers this has proven difficult at times. During the dark days indoctrination was nigh on impossible and bordering on child cruelty. In fact, even for adults watching County in the dark days was masochistic at times. Fortunately, nights like tonight do the job for me. The atmosphere was electric with all four sides of EP chanting and cheering. When we scored, strangers were hugging each other. Inhibitions gone in an involuntary show of joy.

All the players performed well. Hats off to Francis-Angol for coming into such a key match and performing well after such a long time out. Newby just kept having a go down the wing. Sarcevic was great in the middle pinging passes and Cannon was the missing ingredient we needed. Paddy Madden, goal scorer and man of the match, ran his socks off. He plays as if he has supported County all his life. Hinchliffe- another clean sheet, another solid performance. Hippolyte- great again and must be the one our best signings ever. Too many to mention really.

The first half was a story of relentless attacking and close misses including goal line clearances and great saves. Collar was denied on the line by a defender and the Gulls keeper McDonald made a great save with his leg from Madden. Even with all the positivity around our display, we hadn't scored. In recent matches we have dominated periods of matches without scoring and then conceded. Even if we score and with all our domination, Torquay will just need to scramble a goal to ruin our night and possibly our title hopes. It felt like our stars may not be aligned. If the first half display was good our second half pressure was relentless but Torquay were resilient. I asked myself, why are Torquay playing like their lives depend on it? Professionalism I suppose plus a good manager in Gary Johnson.

As chance after chance went wide, high or were saved I was almost settling for a point and resigned to having to get three points from Halifax on Sunday. Fortunately, our talisman delivered again. Just after the hour we finally got a break that by-passed the packed Gulls defence and opened space for Madden to tap in from a Newby cross from the right. For not the first time this season the ground erupted in celebration. One guy came down our row hugging everyone. We jumped up and down arms aloft as if we had scored the winner in the World Cup Final. It was just as important as that goal means we only need a point at home to Halifax on Sunday even if Wrexham win.

There was nearly half an hour left though, so we had a lot to do. The plan was to keep attacking and get a second goal and a bit of a cushion. We didn't start to hold the ball up until the last few minutes. We kept going for the second goal which worked in the end. If we had gone defensive and tried to kill the game we would have allowed Torquay to apply pressure. Somehow ex-County keeper Halstead deflected a Hippolyte effort over from close range. Halstead replaced the injured McDonald at half time. Both keepers were excellent. On another day we would be three or four up. Then, as we approached a precious three points, late drama saw Wynter head the ball on to our crossbar. If that would have gone in, even a neutral would have judged it as an injustice.

With four minutes of added time complete, the ref finally blew his whistle. The ground erupted again. People hugged each other; others punched the air. The players congratulated each other, Challinor came on to the pitch. The collective clapped the fans in a mutual show of appreciation. A magical County moment for sure. Up there with some of the greatest matches at EP. Walking back to the car the atmosphere was buzzing as fans savoured the victory. I had a spring in my step. The County conversion therapy may be working!

Sunday 15th May 2022
County 2   Halifax 0

So, this is it. The last match of the regular season. After ninety minutes we may be in the play-offs. Or we may be victorious and Champions of the National League. Resulting in a return to the Football League and the Holy Grail. It's been eleven long years of non-league football. Most of it an endurance contest. Some fans lost faith. Some couldn't bare it. Some left and came back. Fortunately, a new generation of fans started following us. Fans that have never seen us play in the Football League. Hats off to them. Far easier to be a United fan, then more recently a City fan. But no, they decided to follow their local team. These are the youngsters that organise and take part in the fan marches. I have nothing but respect for these younger fans.

Then again, as I travel the country to various non-league outposts. To the South Coast, West Country, Norfolk, sometimes on a Tuesday night, I see the same faces. Some have been going for over forty years. Some are gregarious and have the banter, some stick to themselves and their mates. Some are active on social media; some keep a lower profile. I see some of these loyalists in pubs around the town. Some have a mutual interest in music and go to pub gigs. These are the faces of County. A loyal breed. Through thick and thin. Then again, some can't get to a lot of the matches due to work and family commitments. But they share the same passion. This all makes the good times sweeter. The County community. This season they are being rewarded for all their loyalty.

I have checked out the permutations for today's final matches of the season. If our opponents do better than Solihull they could go third meaning they go straight to the play-off semi-finals. They will be desperate for the win. So a big challenge for us to gain that magical point or three. Wrexham are away at Dagenham. If the Daggers win and Chesterfield lose then they sneak into the play-offs ahead of the Spireites.

So conversely, a big task for our Welsh challengers. All four teams in the two games have everything to play for. Wrexham need to win. I'm an honorary Daggers fan for the day.

It's all in our own hands still and advantage to County. Prior to kick-off a truly impressive display is going on in the Cheadle End. The Hatters 83 Supporters Group have organised the array of flags and banners that cover the stand and individual colour cards to create the display. This is the group that also organise the pre-match marches. This type of choreographed display is known as a Tifo on the continent. Our Tifo is just our fans and loads of great County flags and banners. Crystal Palace do something similar but theirs is more of a copy of the overseas style. Plus they have lots of fans dressed in black. I prefer ours.

With the league going down to the last day a set of medals and a trophy are at both venues. Edgeley Park and Dagenham. It's us or The Red Dragons that will be victorious. We won the National North in 18/19 on that glorious day away at Nuneaton. This time the opportunity awaits to win in it at home and lift the trophy at our hallowed ground. Nuneaton was our first trophy for fifty-two years. We've had many great play-off wins but securing a trophy took a while (I guess our 2016 and 2022 Cheshire Cup wins don't count as a fully first team cup). We've won several minor cups just in case any County historians are reading. In 66/67 we had already won the Fourth Division by the final home game. So, today provides a unique opportunity in the history of Stockport County. To win the league at home and lift the trophy on the same day in front of our homes fans.

The tension built up for many the whole week before kick-off but I was strangely relaxed. I'd seen enough in our last match against Torquay to readjust my confidence compass. Midweek we got our mojo back or more specifically our midfield. With the exception of Madden, some teams have two great strikers. However, we have by far the best midfield. Cannon, Collar, Croasdale and Sarcevic are the four best midfielders in the league and we have all of them. Supplement that with Hippolyte, Keane and latterly Francis-Angol plus our wider options including Newby, Crankshaw etc and we have a formidable combo. Today, all these player came to the fore creating link up play the Shaymen couldn't handle.

More of that later. Pre-match there was a magnificent display in the Cheadle End. At the bottom behind the goal running almost the full width of the pitch was an Animo Et Fide, Courage and Faith banner. The motto of County and Stockport or the family that originally ruled the roost around these parts. Then in all the seats they had coloured cards that were held up to form a fan of blue and white. From my angle in the Pop Side I presumed it read SCFC but it transpired to be a fan of colour that looked brilliant. The chants started. The crowd of 10,300 included about 900 Halifax fans in the Railway End. Quite a few empty seats which was a bit disappointing for them. The Pop Side was all County and the atmosphere electric.

Keeping a similar line up as last time against the Gulls with the Keane/Angol/Palmer back three and the fantastic four in midfield, County looked quality. The one touch passing was top notch and Halifax couldn't win the ball in the centre of the park. The only time they regained control was in the rare event that we gave the ball away. Supplemented with the effervescent Newby and now legendary Madden the Shaymen couldn't cope with our energy. Even ex-County legend Matty Warburton struggled to get into the game for the opposition.

After just ten minutes we made the breakthrough when Sarcevic fed Paddy who fizzed the ball into the net from close range. That was his twenty-fifth goal of the season. That goal tally plus his outstanding work rate and likeability has earned our number nine legendary status amongst the fanbase. If anyone epitomises this promotion campaign it is Paddy Madden. There are many other heroes but Paddy shades it as player of the year. From that early moment, a belief swept over the stadium. We can do this. This is our League and we will be Champions this afternoon.

Fifteen minutes later our captain Madden curled a shot onto the crossbar. Cannon had a great shot tipped over the bar and then news filtered through that Dagenham had scored. Later on it transpired that the goal was disallowed. But the Daggers scored three second half goals to thwart Wrexham's challenge on our league title. The half time break involved lots of excitable chatter about how close we are to winning the league. Confidence levels were sky high. From nervousness and panic for some after the Wrexham defeat we seemed to have turned everything around in the last two games. Rediscovered our form and confidence. We've had plenty of possession recently but the goal return had dried up somewhat. Now, we look like scoring again.

After only nine minutes of the restart a Cannon thunderbolt was parried into the path of Collar who fired home. The party was getting started even before the news from East London that Wrexham had conceded one, then two goals. After all the nail-biting of recent weeks it seemed like this was too good to be true. But no, this was well deserved. We probably should have won this league a few weeks ago. Today it all fell into place. The stars are aligned and these players are getting their just deserts. We continued to ping the ball around like worthy champions. A class above a decent Halifax side.

With the fans nearly on the pitch before the final whistle blew a magical event was going down in County history. A full stadium of passionate fans ready to celebrate with the players who are about to achieve a return to the Football League after eleven long years. All captured live on national TV too for me to peruse later, tomorrow and probably several other times over the summer. The ref finally gave a signal to his linesmen to leg it before blowing the whistle. A wave of humanity then ran across the pitch to celebrate with the players. We stood for a few minutes before walking onto the pitch to take some celebratory photos. Many had ran to the dugouts and lifted players on their shoulders. Our heroes punched the air as they were carried by fans.

As the friendly melee subsided, players walked around the pitch taking photos with fans. It took a while to clear the pitch. A trophy back drop was erected in the centre circle. Mark Stott and County President Steve Bellis entered the fray. The medals were given out before the trophy was lifted with rapturous applause. Club captain Hogan and captain for the match Madden led the way around the pitch with the trophy. A magical moment. Reward for hard graft. A return to the promised land after eleven years in non-league. Old-timers stood calm but with proud expressions. Some will have seen the 66/67 Championship winners. Young fans knee-slid across the turf.

Eventually the crowd dispersed. Some onto Castle Street to celebrate in the pubs. Some calmly back home. No doubt many will watch it back on TV tonight or tomorrow or this week. I'm sure many will replay it this summer. Wrexham's challenge was a good challenge towards the end but I enjoyed checking the league table. It says we finished six points ahead with a four better goal difference. A swing in the last week but the table looks realistic now. We are the best team in the league by at least six points.

Wrexham's Hollywood owners tweeted post-match. Ryan Reynolds congratulated County. He wasn't sure of the "math" but he knew they'd been in a scrap with the best team. Nice comment. The math is that they are in the play-offs. Meanwhile his cohort Rob McElhenney posted- lets dust ourselves off and go finish it. Whatever their knowledge is, these guys deserve credit for investing themselves in English/Welsh football at this level. A much nicer and more genuine story than some of the Premier League investors.

This is where it all ends for now. Thousands of miles travelled. An amazing season resulting in a return to the League. So many great player performances and an absolutely amazing managerial appointment in Dave Challinor. A destiny changing influence from Mark Stott. Highs, a few lows and many proud moments created by the players and supporters. I set out pre-lockdown to follow this team to as many games as possible and that was somewhat scuppered due to a pandemic. We failed at the play-off semi-final stage. This time we actually did it with the fans back in the ground. I've thoroughly enjoyed it. But it's time now for a cold celebratory beer! WE'RE BACK! And thank you very much for reading this report on a magnificent season. As the brilliant Dave Challinor would say- Cheers, Thank you!

Epilogue

So there you have it. Another season in the history of by far the greatest team the world has ever seen. Stockport County AFC of course. Eleven years ago we were relegated into non-league. A quick demise after winning the League Two play-offs in 2008. We ran out of money. Back-to-back relegations saw us drop out of the Football League for the first time in over 100 years. We were fined twice and had points deducted for financial transgressions. Our stadiums owner only cared about rugby and was ready to sell the ground to developers leaving us homeless. Fortunately, the council stepped in and bought the ground. Without any assets and diminishing match day revenue the future was uncertain.

In our first year in the National League we nearly went down for the third year in a row. The next season we went down into regional football in 2012/13. We had four managers that season in what had become a complete shambles. One of those situations whereby you don't know whether to laugh or cry. We went part-time to save money. In theory this status would attract the better part-time players. It didn't work. The club spent an unbelievably baffling six seasons in the National North. We had become a mid-table team in regional non-league football. County fans call them the dark days.

Jim Gannon and an improving squad of players eventually got us out of the mire and back into the top division in non-league by winning the National North in 2018/19. We had hovered over the precipice and dropped further than any other team in the history of football apart from the ones that went bust. But the heartbeat never stopped. Hard core fans remained and youngsters started following the club in its darkest days. Gallows humour helped and visits to characterful and sometimes bizarre non-league outposts somehow entered into County folklore. Even at our nadir there were still many Hatters fans following the team in a sometimes-masochistic show of loyalty.

Then came a saviour in January 2020. Mr Stott. Our local super successful businessman and investor in his local football club. Not necessarily a full-on County fan but a sympathiser and good intentioned philanthropist. We now have a 250-year lease of Edgeley Park and are debt free with a sustainable plan to climb the divisions. It literally was like winning the jackpot on the lottery. The pandemic threw another curve ball and the appointment of Rusk as manager ended in an underwhelming play-off semi-final defeat in 2020/21. Rusk hung on before the decision makers decided enough was enough as we languished in tenth position at the end of October 2021.

The club decided to go for a tried and trusted achiever at this level and appointed Dave Challinor as manager. The messiah you may say. An unbelievably successful run of results re-wrote the County record books. The most wins in a season. The longest winning streaks. The longest runs without defeat. The most points in a season. The list went on. From tenth to top in two months then a relentless stay at the top.

I travelled over six thousand miles following the Hatters this season missing only a few matches home and away in all competitions. Sometimes involving long distance journey's followed by other long-distance journeys in the same week with work. Bromley away then up to Newcastle and Woking away then over to Somerset being two mileage accumulating examples. I said I'd make as many games as possible. I missed a few. Dover away being a match too far as I'd just come back from visiting my eldest son at Uni up in Newcastle.

Fortunately, as soon as Dave Challinor took over in November 21 we have been brilliant. What a pleasure it has been to follow the team and share the experience with County fans and my two sons live. Also, to share the tales with my wife and daughter on my return from the regular excursions. Kath often queried the frequency of my absences as I left for a mid-week match a few of days after another long-distance away journey. I assured her that following a team in all the cups and the league does add up!

In the end we did it. Wrexham pushed us hard on the final furlong but County came out on top. On top of the league and champions. A return to the Football League and the Holy Grail. This season certainly pushed 96/97 close as the best season ever. Maybe it is the best season ever. Certainly in the sense of the monumental effort and achievement of getting out of non-league. The National League has to be one of the most competitive leagues to get out of. With only one automatic promotion place the difficulty factor is immense.

This season has to be the best ever in terms of the re-birth of the County supporters. Not only in numbers but the passionate response to the teams valiant efforts. The players to a man have been brilliant and invested in the club and supporters. There has been a bond there which is awesome to be a part of. Looking back, highlights include the two games against Bolton and the Rotherham game in the FA Cup where we went toe to toe against League 1 opposition. The away following of over 5,000 at Bolton. Then there have been numerous massive crowds in the league games and amazing atmospheres. The County hard-core have always been great but the overall support from the fans this season has been particularly memorable.

Thank you for reading this dedication to our 21/22 season. I hope you have enjoyed it. I'm going for a lie down now in preparation for next season!

Acknowledgements

Thank you!

Bob Thompson - life-long County fan – cheers for the kind words about the first book and suggesting a "sequel."

Kath & Jonnie - wife & youngest son- for listening to my County pontifications apart from most Saturday's and Tuesday's (when I'm at the match, although Jonnie joins me a lot).

Will & Daniela - eldest son and daughter – Will at Uni and Daniela lives in London- away from home but still get the County updates and sound interested (I think)! But I do ask them how they are doing first of course.

Stockport County ticket office - for all your friendly assistance.

Ian "hedgegrower" Brown – thank you for the use of your photo's on the cover.

Ed Powell - for inviting me to promote the last book "Back Next Year" at the Stockport Programme & Memorabilia Fair.

Ruben Clark - the writer following County, Ashton United and Mossley for a book about the non-league football community. Inspirational stuff.

Mike Bayly - providing inspiration with his brilliant photographs and reports in his book- British Football's Greatest Grounds.

And last but not least- anyone else I've chatted with, laughed with, held my head with, sang with and celebrated with this season.

Also by the author...

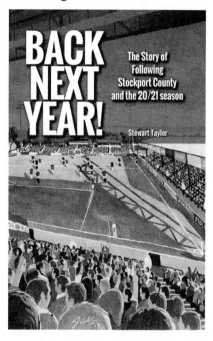

From the lone County fan at Guiseley to the play-off semi-final against Hartlepool, Stewart Taylor went to every length to follow Stockport County in 20/21. The massive curve ball of a pandemic cramped his ambition to attend every match, but by hook or by crook, every game was viewed: by live stream or in the ground, through official ticket or innocent blag.

The most challenging of seasons is documented match by match with anecdotes from past and present County matches, tinged with the gallows humour required to follow a lower league club over decades. You can laugh, cry, reminisce and celebrate the joys and pains shared at the County church of football. Ultimately, the story ends in disappointment but the future looks bright. County are on the way back. The journey is just starting and we'll be back next year!

Buy online at victorpublishing.co.uk

Also available from Victor Publishing...

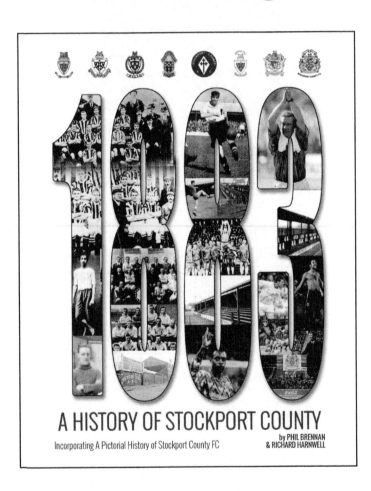

A HISTORY OF STOCKPORT COUNTY

Incorporating A Pictorial History of Stockport County FC

by PHIL BRENNAN
& RICHARD HARNWELL

Buy online at victorpublishing.co.uk

Danny came, he saw, he conquered. He made a lasting impression on all his friends and colleagues as a canny football coach in a foreign country. He could trap, he could volley, he could shoot - he could bend the ball years before Beckham did. - David Pleat

Today we happily accommodate Premier League managers speaking through an interpreter - even an England boss in the early days of Fabio Capello - Danny was a pioneer in going on to become the first Football League manager not to speak English as a first language. The Uruguayan went the extra mile to learn it, unlike so many who have followed him. Yet he was given all too little credit for that. - Alan Biggs

I really liked Danny as a man first and foremost. I thought he was one of the best people I have ever worked with in football and it goes without saying that he had a real talent when it came to spotting a player. - Mick McCarthy

Buy online at victorpublishing.co.uk

Also available from
Victor Publishing...

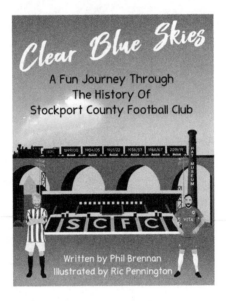

Clear Blue Skies - A Fun Journey Through The History of Stockport County Football Club

Having started out their journey as Heaton Norris Rovers, Stockport County Football Club have a long and proud history in English Football.

Thanks to the town's hat-making prowess the club were given the nickname 'The Hatters' early on in their history.

Since the club was founded it has set several Football League records that still stand today whilst also winning several titles, regional cup competitions and p;laying at Wembley Stadium on five occasions.

This is a fun journey through the club's history aimed at an ever-growing young fanbase at Edgeley Park, Stockport County's home since 1902...

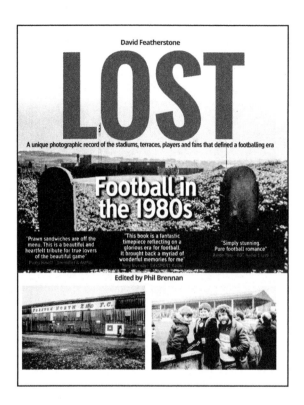

The 1980s are remembered as a bleak time in the history of English football. Dismissed as a time the game was blighted by hooliganism and tragedy.

Since the advent of the Premier League in 1992, it's easy to forget that going to the match before then was still a hugely enjoyable experience, accessible and affordable to all.

With new, modern, often soulless, identikit stadiums now commonplace, also forgotten are the unique stands, terraces, facades and features that gave every club its own identity.

This book unearths a huge, previously unseen treasure trove of images from that forgotten era.

An era that was, until now, lost.

Buy online at victorpublishing.co.uk

Coming soon...

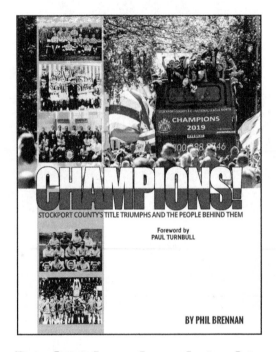

Revised and updated to commemorate Stockport County's return to the Football League as National League Champions

Got a book in you?

PUBLISHING
victorpublishing.co.uk

This book is published by Victor Publishing.

Victor Publishing specialises in getting new and independent writers' work published worldwide in both paperback and Kindle format.

We also look to re-publish titles that were previously published but have now gone out of circulation or off-sale.

If you have a manuscript for a book (or have previously published a now off-sale title) of any genre (fiction, non-fiction, autobiographical, biographical or even reference or photographic/illustrative) and would like more information on how you can get your work published and on sale in print and digitally, please visit us at: www.victorpublishing.co.uk or get in touch at: enquiries@victorpublishing.co.uk

Printed in Great Britain
by Amazon